D1706943

TheoPhostic

Counseling

Divine Revelation?

or

PsychoHeresy?

Martin & Deidre Bobgan

EastGate Publishers
Santa Barbara, CA 93110

The Scriptures in the quotes from Dr. Ed Smith are those selected and used by him. All Scriptures not quoted from Smith are from the King James Version of the Bible.

Grammatical errors made by Smith are neither corrected nor signified in this critique.

For a sample copy of a free newsletter about the intrusion of psychological counseling theories and therapies into the church, please write to:

PsychoHeresy Awareness Ministries
4137 Primavera Road
Santa Barabara, CA 93110

TheoPhostic Counseling:
Divine Revelation or Psychoheresy?

Copyright © 1999 Martin and Deidre Bobgan
Published by EastGate Publishers
Santa Barbara, CA 93110

Library of Congress Catalog Card Number 99-91321
ISBN 0-941717-15-1

Printed in the United States of America

CONTENTS

1

TheoPhostic Counseling: Latter-Day Revelation from God?

Over the past two years people have been asking us, "Do you know anything about TheoPhostic counseling?" Initially we had not heard of TheoPhostic counseling. After all, there are so many names of different combinations of counseling techniques that one can hardly keep track of them. However, as these questions began coming more frequently and even from other countries, our curiosity was aroused. In a brief article in the *PsychoHeresy Awareness Letter* we asked for information from our readers and wrote, "We would appreciate learning more about TheoPhostic counseling."[1] Because of information received from readers, we were able to obtain both written and audio cassette information from Dr. Ed M. Smith, the originator of the TheoPhostic system. After reading Smith's written information and listening to his tapes, we decided to evaluate his counseling system and make the information available to others.

We begin our evaluation by directly quoting from the manual used at Smith's conferences:

5

The word *TheoPhostic* is a term I created from two Greek words. It comes from the combination of the Greek words *Theos* (God) and *Phos* (light). These two terms describe God bringing forth illumination into a previously darkened area of one's mind. *TheoPhostic* counseling offers a new and revolutionary means of accomplishing what traditional approaches to therapy I only saw produce in facsimile.

Does this mean we have to throw away all we have gained as therapists? Absolutely not! But it will require a major shift in our thinking and normal procedures. It will require us to move from believing *about* the miraculous to believing *in* miracles.

TheoPhostic counseling is a process of divinely accomplished miracles. In its simplest description, it is merely exposing darkness with light. It is the revealing of truth, freeing the individual of the lies which dominate their thinking, emotions and behavior. It sets people free from lifelong fears, shame, false guilt, and anxiety, lifting the dark clouds of depression *in an instant*.[2] (Italics his.)*

Smith describes how TheoPhostic counseling came to him after a session with "a group of ladies who were all members of our 'Adult survivors of Sexual Abuse support group'" (p. 30). He says:

As I drove home that night I asked God to show me a way to quicken this process of shifting from

---

* From this point on, all page references in the text refer to the manual titled *Beyond Tolerable Recovery: Moving beyond tolerable existence, into genuine restoration and emotional inner healing. TheoPhostic Counseling* by Ed M. Smith. Throughout the remainder of our critique, all italics and other forms of emphasis in material quoted from Smith are his unless otherwise indicated.

embracing the lie to knowing the truth. I did not receive an answer that evening in the car but over the course of the next few weeks a simple yet profound principle began to emerge. It was as though a spigot had been turned on and the insight of this process began to flow through my mind (p. 30).

Smith claims God gave TheoPhostic counseling to him. He says, "After I had searched long and hard for that 'better' method, He [God] gave me *TheoPhostic* so I would have no room to boast" (p. 31). Smith tells in detail and with the use of metaphors how "God was revealing this method to me" (p. 32). Elsewhere in the manual Smith refers to "God's gift of *TheoPhostic* therapy" (p. 17).

A common experience of authors and publishers is listening to someone who has written a poem, article or book say, "God gave me," "God revealed to me," "God showed me," or some similar phrase and then ask, "What do you think?" What can the response be? If God truly revealed to the person what he is presenting, what can the respondee say? If the response to the piece is critical, it comes across as criticizing God, because, after all, the person claims God gave or revealed it.

One is placed in a similar position with TheoPhostic counseling. If God did reveal it to Smith, there is nothing more to say. God is perfect and what He reveals is perfectly true. If the supporter of TheoPhostic counseling believes this method came directly from God, that ends the discussion. Why would he read this or any other critique about it? For him, it would be tantamount to questioning God's revelation. However, Scripture says, "Beloved, believe not every spirit, but try the spirits whether they are of God: because many false prophets are gone out into the world" (1 John 4:1). This means that Christians are to discern the source of teaching, whether it is from God or from the influence of deceiving spirits.

When a person claims to have received teachings, principles or methods from God, Christians have a duty to be like the Bereans, who were commended because they "searched the scriptures daily, whether those things were so" (Acts 17:11). Believers are to "prove all things; hold fast that which is good" (1 Thes. 5:21). Moreover, believers are to confront error and expose it (Galatians 2:11-14). It is actually biblically irresponsible not to examine the teachings of those who claim to have a direct revelation from God.

Our purpose in writing this critique is to "try the spirits." We hope and pray that others will also critique TheoPhostic counseling, because there are some facets of it we are not covering. Our critique is for those who need proof regarding whether what Smith says is divine revelation. Smith makes certain biblical, psychological, personal and scientific-sounding statements that need to be put to the test. Is Smith's system, and that's what we believe it is, true to Scripture, and is the information he gives accurate and supported in the scientific literature?

Smith says, "I have been doing therapy in many different forms and settings for over twenty years" (p. 31). During this period of time Smith confesses, "I believe He [God] wanted me to try every available method of therapy being offered in our country" (p. 31). Note the "every available method of therapy" and note the length of time, "for over twenty years," and then think about the many people Smith subjected to ungodly forms of psychotherapy. Does that sound like something God would have someone do?

Smith refers to TheoPhostic counseling as given by God: "He gave me *TheoPhostic* so I would have no room to boast" (p. 31), and he says he has been using TheoPhostic counseling since February, 1996 (p. 142). He also refers to it as "therapy" when he says, "I believe this gift of therapy will become just another part of the total healing God is accomplishing throughout" (p. 31).

The following is a brief description of TheoPhostic theory and practice: Present problems are due to past (usually early-life) events, early interpretations of those events ("lies"), and their accompanying emotions. The "lies," which drive present thinking, feeling, and behaving, are embedded in early-life memories, located in the "dark room," which must be accessed through "drifting" into the past in search of early "memory pictures" that feel the same as the negative feeling accompanying the present problematic situation. During this search, the client is encouraged to find Jesus and describe what he is doing and saying. Once the memory holding the "original lie" has been located, the therapist must identify the "lie" (e.g., "I'm bad," "It's my fault," "I'm worthless"). Then comes "stirring the darkness," which involves having the client repeat the "lie" over and over again to intensify his emotions and prepare him to hear God speak "truth" directly to him, thereby replacing the darkness with "light."

Is TheoPhostic a divine, latter-day revelation from God as Smith claims, or is it a Smith-devised variation of one or more of the many psychotherapies he learned and used, to which he added inner healing concepts and techniques?

During the past twenty-five years we have investigated and evaluated the therapies of some of the most popular psychologizers of the faith. Some of their approaches are, by their own admission, taken directly from secular psychological sources. However, very often the true secular sources of their therapies are disguised. The secular originators, their techniques and theories, and their most important ideas, while used, are not identified by many who claim to be Christian therapists.

Most psychotherapists who profess Christianity are as eclectic as their secular counterparts. Eclecticism, which involves blending two or more psychological approaches, is so widely used by therapists to describe what they do that the *Handbook of Psychotherapy and Behavior Change* reports, "Therapists identify themselves as eclectics more frequently than any other orientation."[3] Likewise, Smith has borrowed ideas and techniques from several psychotherapeutic systems. However, he might deny being eclectic and does claim that TheoPhostic counseling "is *not* a spin-off of any other traditional approach to counseling."[4] Smith names several psychotherapy approaches and claims that TheoPhostic is **not** like any of them.

Even though Smith claims TheoPhostic counseling was the result of direct, divine revelation from God, we will demonstrate that TheoPhostic is more likely a Smith-contrived, eclectic therapy that came from his "over twenty year" practice as a psychotherapist using "every available method of therapy." While TheoPhostic is not totally like any one psychotherapy, it is the sum of a variety of therapies and techniques, kaleidoscopically assembled together with known inner healing ideas and practices along with imaginative additions, which include redescribing techniques and redefining terms. TheoPhostic is unique, but primarily in its patchwork approach, which is different from any other eclectic mixture we have seen. However, TheoPhostic's major elements originated from known psychotherapies and inner healing practices and these sources can easily be identified.

Smith says he wondered why God would give him such a revelation as TheoPhostic and reports:

> My wife Sharon believes the reason was a simple one. She said to me, "The reason He gave this process to you was because you asked." Could it be that simple? Did I "have not" simply because I "ask not"?
>
> The bottom line is, I asked and He gave, and I am grateful and willing to share it with those who will listen.[5]

In describing this revelation, Smith says:

> Before God blessed me with *TheoPhostic* counseling, much of what is in this book had never passed through my mind. As I was open to learning a new approach God began to pour this information into my mind. . . . **I could not write down the new information fast enough to keep up with what God was saying to me** (pp. 164, 165). (Bold added.)

These words are reminiscent of such books as *God Calling* and *A Course in Miracles*, in which the writers claim to have received revelation directly from God or Jesus.

Please note that Smith refers to what he believes God gave him as "new information" and says, "much of what is in this book had never passed through my mind." We will demonstrate that TheoPhostic counseling is NOT "new information" to Smith and that much of what he does reflects the various psychotherapies he admittedly knew and practiced for "over twenty years."

TheoPhostic counseling is the result of many existent therapies, including psychoanalytic, Eye Movement Desensitization and Reprocessing (EMDR), and cognitive-behavioral therapies. In addition, TheoPhostic includes elements from the inner healing movement, which includes guided imagery, visualization, and hypnosis. **As a result of our analysis we conclude that TheoPhostic counseling came out of the evil cauldron of the perverted wisdom of men rather than from the mind of God.** We present our reasons for this, our comparisons with what appear to be Smith's sources, and a concern about how he misuses Scripture to support TheoPhostic counseling.

Notes:

[1] *PsychoHeresy Awareness Letter*, Vol. 7, No. 1, p. 8.

[2] Ed M. Smith. *Beyond Tolerable Recovery: Moving beyond tolerable existence, into genuine restoration and emotional inner healing. TheoPhostic Counseling.* Campbellsville, KY: Family Care Publishing, 1996, p. 11. **From this point on all page references in the text refer to this manual.**

[3] Allen E. Bergin and Sol L. Garfield, eds. *Handbook of Psychotherapy and Behavior Change*, Fourth Edition. New York: John Wiley & Sons, Inc., 1994, p. 7.
[4] Ed M. Smith. "Breakthroughs in Biblical Counseling and Genuine Inner Healing." FAX regarding TheoPhostic Training Seminars, Campbellsville, KY, p. 4.
[5] Edward M. Smith. *Genuine Recovery: Recoverer's guide to true inner healing and renewal of the mind.* Campbellsville, KY: Alathia Inc., 1996, p. 4.

2

TheoPhostic Claims, Cures, and Cases

The TheoPhostic counseling manual is filled with claims, cures, and cases, but NO verifiable proof as to its effectiveness. To demonstrate the extravagant, extreme, and extraordinary claims, cures, and cases, we provide quotes from the TheoPhostic manual in several categories. There will be some overlap, but the overall effect will reveal the extremity of the TheoPhostic claims for cures.

Extremity of Claims

The extremity of the extravagant claims are seen throughout the TheoPhostic manual. Entire sentences will not always be used, but one can check the original context from the page references following the quotations.

I am speaking of complete release . . . (p. 4).

If you learn these principles and apply them as suggested in this book, you will see dynamic results; guaranteed! (p. 5).

. . . she was healed completely . . . (p. 8).

. . . complete healing of the memory being dealt with (p. 15).

. . . instantaneous release . . . (p. 19).

No effort is necessary to you to attain it. No effort is required of you to maintain it (pp. 19, 20).

TheoPhostic counseling can make it possible for a person to be relieved totally from all their shame and guilt (p. 41).

Then the outcome [of using TheoPhostic counseling] is always complete recovery (p. 113).

. . . she experienced immediate release from these feelings (p. 127).

In every case thus far, when appropriate confession and repentance is made, people have experienced release and receive divine truth (p. 128).

This same young man who had been emotionally crippled the week before was completely free (p. 140).

Thus far, in every case in our counseling center where these conditions were met, God has spoken. The result is always freedom and healing; *no exceptions!* (p. 150).

. . . amazing results we see with *TheoPhostic* counseling . . . (p. 160).

The word was simple yet totally set him free . . . one word totally changed his life (p. 161).

. . . each one reported complete healing . . . no trace of the residual remained (p. 179).

. . . you can say to your clients, "You are healed!" (p. 192).

Divine Source and Use

According to Smith, TheoPhostic was a divine revelation given directly to him by God. As quoted earlier, Smith says, "I could not write down the new information fast enough to keep up with what God was saying to me" (pp. 164, 165). Smith claims, "*TheoPhostic* counseling works because it is divine" (p. 151). He refers to it as "the avenue for divine healing" (p. 181) and as "divinely powerful" (p. 4). Smith contends that God speaks directly and personally to the mind of the client during the TheoPhostic counseling session. He says, "If God does not speak, nothing will happen. The truly exciting thing is He always speaks" (p. 31).

Smith claims conversions using TheoPhostic counseling and says, "I have led more people to Jesus since *TheoPhostic* than at any other time in my ministry" (pp. 93, 151; similar statement on p. 110). Moreover, Smith believes that God speaks to unbelievers "just as he does his own" (p. 235). Because of this, Smith says, "I have the privilege of introducing people to Jesus on a regular basis" (p. 235).

Cognitive Behavioral Therapy

Smith confesses the similarity of "cognitive therapy" to TheoPhostic counseling when he says the following:

> Therefore recovery should not be understood as the removal or changing of the memory but rather the reinterpretation of the memory by replacing the embedded lie with truth. This is nothing new to most

of you in that it is the essence of what cognitive therapy assumes. Cognitive therapy in theory has some similarity to *TheoPhostic* counseling in that both are in pursuit of replacing the lie with the truth. **The major difference between cognitive therapy and this approach is the expediency and completeness of *TheoPhostic* counseling in achieving recovery as opposed to the slow process of cognitive therapy.** The cognitive approach uses a processive progressive model moving the person slowly along step by step toward becoming better. The strength of cognitive therapy is in the ability of the therapist in discerning the faulty thinking and supplying truth for the client to embrace. The weakness is in how long it takes to arrive at this place (p. 26). (Bold added.)

Regarding cognitive therapies, the *Handbook of Psychotherapy and Behavior Change* reveals:

Most of the people who used to consider themselves behavioral therapists now identify themselves as cognitive-behavioral. Also, most people who once considered themselves strictly cognitive practitioners now are willing to take on the cognitive-behavioral label as well.[1]

However, the *Concise Encyclopedia of Psychology* defines "Cognitive Behavior therapy" and "Cognitive therapies" separately. It says:

Cognitive behavior therapy is an approach designed to change mental images, thoughts, and thought patterns so as to help patients overcome emotional and behavioral problems. It is based on the theory that behaviors and emotions are caused in part by cognitions and cognitive processes that one can learn to change.[2]

Cognitive therapies are a loosely associated group of approaches that stress the importance of cognitive processes as determinants of behavior. They maintain that behavior and emotions result largely from one's appraisal of the situation, and that, because appraisal is influenced by beliefs, assumptions, images, and self-talk, these cognitions become the targets of therapy.[3]

There is more than just a similarity between cognitive therapy and TheoPhostic; cognitive therapy is one of the many therapies that comprise the source of Smith's TheoPhostic system.

Brief, Brief Therapy

Prior to his supposed revelation from God, Smith confesses, "Before *TheoPhostic*, I was used to spending years with a client dealing with the strongholds I faced" (p. 239). Smith repeats this idea in several places. He says, "What used to take years to accomplish using traditional means, we now see in only a few sessions" (p. 10). He also says, "I have literally seen more progress in one session with some clients than I have seen in years of sessions using my former traditional approaches" (p. 213).

Smith not only examined and used traditional therapies, but he also looked into "Brief therapy" and says:

I did look into the theories of "Brief Therapy" and learned some things that did enhance and quicken the recovery process. But when God blessed me with *TheoPhostic* counseling I began to witness something which went far beyond "brief" (p. 139).

Smith amplifies this in other places in the manual. He says, "Even the current so called 'brief therapy' is slow compared to the instantaneous release found using *TheoPhostic* counseling" (p. 26). The extent of Smith's claim for "brief" is seen in the following:

> The advantages of using *TheoPhostic* counseling are many. Primarily, it goes quickly to the root of the person's trouble, bringing *instant* release and healing. No, this is not a typing error. I did say *instant* (p. 11).

> *TheoPhostic* counseling provides instant release and recovery . . . (p. 33).

> I am excited that Christian counselors have a divinely dynamic method [TheoPhostic] of helping people find instant release from the painful memories that bind them (p. 109).

> If the truth is spoken there will be immediate results of freedom (p. 113).

Smith repeatedly testifies to the supposed rapidity of healing using his TheoPhostic method, as seen in the following quotations:

> All of this occurred in the course of 35 minutes (p. 24).

> *TheoPhostic* counseling provides instant release and recovery . . . (p. 33).

> Some [eating disorders] are cured in as little as one session (pp. 53, 54).

After you have done *TheoPhostic* counseling for awhile you will come to expect great outcomes in a single session (p. 95).

Carl gained complete freedom from the lies and depressing emotions in the first session after he heard the truth (p. 106).

Complete recovery of the pain from sexual abuse had occurred in the course of a fifty-minute session (p. 140).

Without hesitation she said she had received far more recovery in this session than she had received in the entire five years [in traditional therapy] (p. 214).

In addition to TheoPhostic's brevity with a variety of problems, Smith also used it for Dissociative Identity Disorder (DID). Smith claims, "We have had great results using *TheoPhostic* counseling with DID and have seen complete recovery in a short amount of time in cases thus far" (p. 79). He adds, "I have personally witnessed (and recorded) cases of persons with Multiple Personality or DID who have been completely restored in a short amount of time: one in only six hours" (p. 79).

"Genuine Recovery" versus "Tolerable Recovery"

Smith contrasts what he calls "genuine recovery" with "tolerable recovery." "Genuine recovery" is what is accomplished using TheoPhostic counseling; "tolerable recovery" is what other therapeutic approaches offer and what Smith says he offered prior to his "divine" revelation of TheoPhostic (pp. 17-29). Smith equates *genuine recovery* and *TheoPhostic* counseling throughout the manual. For example, he says, "Genuine recovery is freedom from the lies that control and dictate such behavior. *TheoPhostic* counseling will accomplish this" (p. 32). Under "Tolerable Recovery" Smith says, "The person was taught how . . . they could live their lives at a tolerable level" (p. 282).

Bottom Line

Smith refers to himself as a "'bottom line' counselor" (p. 113), and the bottom line for Smith is that TheoPhostic works. He says:

> Once you try this method and watch the dramatic change which occurs in the life of the one you are working with, you will realize the awesome validity of *TheoPhostic* counseling (p. 85).

Smith declares that the large numbers claimed to be set free are proof that it works. He says, "This method does work and has set thousands of people free in ways I have never seen in all the years I have been doing therapy" (p. 90). Smith declares, "*TheoPhostic* counseling works because it is divine" (p. 94).

Predictability

While most psychotherapies do not contain predictions as to outcomes, TheoPhostic does. After speaking about "instant release" from such life-impacting emotions as "pain, shame, guilt and fear," Smith declares, "It is possible and predictable using *TheoPhostic* counseling" (p. 12). Compared to traditional therapy, Smith says, "I believe the difference with *TheoPhostic* counseling is it is a predictable method which, when used correctly, **always works**" (pp. 30, 31). (Bold added.)

Changes Using Smith's TheoPhostic Method

Another spectacular claim by Smith is about the permanency of change wrought by TheoPhostic counseling. Smith makes such claims throughout his manual about the permanency of the change with only a few qualifiers.

He says:

> Genuine recovery is divine and relapse is not possible
> . . . (p. 18).

> Thus far, all people have maintained and improved
> from their original ratings with no regression what-
> soever (p. 105).

> Thus far, we have had no one report having received
> a spirit again after it had been expelled (p. 209).

In a chapter titled "Evidence of true healing," Smith
lists the following five evidences:

1. True healing is permanent . . . (p. 141).

2. True healing results in lifestyle change . . . (p. 145).

3. Healing provides the power to confront the
   monsters in our lives . . . (p. 146).

4. True healing impacts one's present relationships
   . . . (p. 147).

5. True healing does not require any effort to maintain . . . (p. 148).

In each of these sections Smith testifies to the effectiveness of TheoPhostic counseling.

Ease of Learning

TheoPhostic counseling is easy to learn and easy to
practice. It can be learned in one brief workshop and then
practiced. Smith gives an example of just how easy it is to
learn and use:

A Pastor friend of mine, Rev. Greg Elkins, had the opportunity to observe me counseling a person using *TheoPhostic* therapy. After this one experience (and not having read this book) he was thrust into a counseling situation that was very traumatic for the person he was dealing with (and maybe for him too) (p. 250).

According to Smith, Elkins took the client (a girl) through the basic steps he had learned by observing Smith in one session. The result? Smith reports that Elkins "said within twenty-five minutes after he had entered the room finding this girl coiled up in a fetal position she was sitting up laughing and in good spirits, free from the trauma that had her immobilized just moments before" (p. 250).

Veiled Disclaimers

In spite of all his extravagant claims and surety of TheoPhostics working, Smith does include some veiled disclaimers along the way. For example, Smith presents disclaimers such as "When the basic conditions are met" (p. 31) and "unless the person deliberately goes against the implanted truth in their souls, which is unlikely" (p. 18). Smith also warns that *"A person may still choose to sin after healing resulting in bondage again"* (p. 151) and that a "person can still choose to return to his former behavior resulting in more pain" (p. 151). Yet, Smith does not hold his TheoPhostic system responsible for any failures. If there is failure, it is attributable to the client because of refusing, resisting, not cooperating, or not continuing the process.

Smith also explains why those who have been set free may think they are afflicted with the same old feelings. He says, "I know it is not a 'return' but rather another lie ready to be expelled" (p. 142). These statements are typical of inner healers who pronounce healing and explain away any results to the contrary.

Antidepressants

Smith's claim with respect to his clients who have been on antidepressant medications is one we have never encountered before in any of the many psychotherapies with which we are familiar. Smith says:

> *One of the wonderful side effects of this new* [TheoPhostic] *process is most persons who have been dependent on antidepressants are usually able to immediately cut back and even discontinue their medications* (p. 64).

Smith expands this claim in another place to include medical care by saying:

> Most people we see who are presently taking pharmaceuticals no longer have any need for medical assistance once the lies are removed using *TheoPhostic* counseling (p. 154).

Cases

In addition to the extravagant claims and cures, Smith provides descriptions of counseling cases. He refers to numerous clients in his manual and tapes. As one reads through the claims and cures, amplified by their application to actual cases, and discovers how easy it is to learn the TheoPhostic system, there is a natural desire to use his method and even to become a devotee. After all, if one can quickly assimilate the TheoPhostic system, one can possibly emulate the purported plethora of successful cases attested to by Smith. What a temptation!

The above claims, taken directly from the TheoPhostic manual, are representative of numerous others made by

Smith in the manual as well as in other places. Is TheoPhostic a divinely revealed, sure-fire method of instant (at times) healing as advertised and promoted by Smith? Or, is TheoPhostic merely a man-made, scientifically faulty, scripturally errant, and error-ridden system?

Again, if one believes Smith received his latter-day revelation directly from God, there is no point in questioning his claims, cures and cases. However, if one decides to put Smith's claims, cures, and cases to the test, it is necessary to use methods generally used to examine other similar claims. After all, how many self-proclaimed, modern-day prophets have testified to hearing directly from God and been found to be false?

Quick Cures and Testimonials

We phoned Smith's TheoPhostic training center in Campbellsville, Kentucky, requested information about the seminars, and received an eleven-page fax advertising the seminars and materials. The first page is titled "Breakthroughs in *Biblical Counseling and* **Genuine** *Inner Healing.*" (Bold added.)

On the first page of the fax, directly beneath the statement, "*People are* **miraculously transformed** *in only a* **few sessions***!*" there is the following testimonial:

> As a medical doctor, I have never seen such a dynamic means of healing people's emotions as I have seen with *TheoPhostic* counseling. I have witnessed with my own eyes people **miraculously transformed** in only a **few sessions**. It is truly a divine healing counseling method. (Bold added.)

The following is on page two of the fax:

> You will discover how to quickly identify the true source of people's emotional pain and bring **quick**

and **lasting** resolve through the use of simple Biblical principles. (Bold added.)

Besides the medical doctor's testimonial on page one of the fax and the quick cures already mentioned above, additional testimonials are given on page three of the fax. The following are excerpts from the fax:

> *TheoPhostic* counseling has. . . truly changed my life.

> Clients who had previously been seen for months are being set free in a few sessions.

> I am watching person after person truly find freedom and release from the pain God never intended for them to carry.

> Through *TheoPhostic* counseling, my fourteen year old adopted daughter was completely set free from the emotional pain of the sexual and ritual abuse inflicted by others prior to her adoption in just two sessions.

> *TheoPhostic* counseling has forever changed the way I will do counseling with individuals and couples.

> I have continually referred my patients to Dr. Smith and have watched what I believe are miraculous cures. [Same medical doctor quoted above.]

> In one three hour session I was completely set free from a 35 year addiction to pornography.

> I was completely relieved of the emotional shame, fear, and pain of the sexual abuse memories I carried all of my life through *TheoPhostic* counseling.

With the ONE session of *TheoPhostic* counseling, ALL the shame and fear left my three very terrible memories and the devastating ugly emotions have not come back.

After just three sessions of *TheoPhostic* counseling, ALL the pain is completely gone from the memory.

. . . in no time our marriage began to improve. Today our marriage is stronger and more fulfilling than we ever thought possible.

. . . in ONE session all the anger, mistrust and pain left the memory . . . It was an absolute miracle.

The claims, cures, and cases of TheoPhostic counseling are admittedly extraordinary. We have been writing and researching the field of psychotherapy for over 25 years. We have read numerous research studies and volumes on research as well as all or parts of numerous books. We have become familiar to some extent with hundreds of therapies and many more techniques. It is very clear to us that almost no extraordinary claims, cures, and cases as presented by TheoPhostics are found in the literature.

The psychotherapies that make such claims are by far the exceptions. One is EMDR (Eye Movement Desensitization and Reprocessing). There are many similarities between TheoPhostic counseling and EMDR, which also makes extraordinary claims, such as:

One of the most exciting aspects of EMDR is seeing how many people are helped and what a high success rate is achieved.[4]

For example, it is vital for people to understand that EMDR may be surprisingly rapid but that it is not simple.[5]

The rapid change in her emotions (no more anxiety) and her behavior (traveling abroad), along with the recognition of the reasons for her distress and a radical change in how she viewed herself and her abilities, are results typical of EMDR.[6]

The changes took place so rapidly, I could *see* them. It was like watching free association at turbo speed.[7] (Italics theirs.)

For the most part, these follow-up interviews showed spectacular results.[8]

. . . depression, phobias, anxiety, stress, low self-esteem, relationship difficulties, and addictions. In the following chapters, I demonstrate that many of these issues can be quickly resolved through EMDR.[9]

With eyes closed and a slight smile, he told me, "It looked like a garden paradise." This was the first time in twenty years that Doug had recalled anything but the horrors of Vietnam.[10]

After we finished using EMDR on this feeling of being "a failure," Tony was able to go back to the first memory and reach a VOC of 7 [rating scale] on the statement, "I can be comfortably in control."[11]

The accelerated learning that takes place with EMDR is not limited to going from dysfunctional to functional behavior. The learning can also go from functional to exceptional. How far can any of us go if we process old memories of failure or humiliation and open the pathways of our brains to the potential of high achievement?[12]

. . . extremely rapid effects of EMDR. . . .[13]

As cases pour in from all over the globe, it has become clear that there are many more common denominators among people and societies than there are differences. The fact that EMDR shows predictable and rapid results when the appropriate protocols and procedures are used indicates that cross-culturally we share physiological responses that can offer a window into the human mind and potential.[14]

After the EMDR session, he reported a feeling of elation and made no further mention of headaches.[15]

After the EMDR session, she felt competent enough to go shopping for the first time in years.[16]

I could scarcely believe my eyes. In place of the withdrawn, silent child I had seen the day before was a smiling, chattering young girl . . . she seemed to have broken through her sense of isolation, and today she continues to be outgoing instead of depressed and withdrawn.[17]

After EMDR, Cynthia's therapist told me, "The attractive, bouncy sixteen-year-old woman with the radiant smile that glowed from a block away as she neared the office on January 17 was a stunning change from the disheveled 'wreck' who shuffled through the door on November 24th." Cynthia had reversed the effects of years of abuse, trauma, depression, and anxiety that had resulted in three recent hospitalizations for suicide attempts.[18]

Few of the over 400 psychotherapeutic approaches make such extreme claims as EMDR does. But, the extent of EMDR claims are easily eclipsed by TheoPhostic claims.

Another extreme example is that of Dr. Arthur Janov, who invented Primal Therapy (PT). Janov claims that PT is a cure-all. He says, "Primal Therapy *should* be able to do away with all symptoms or the premise—that symptoms are the result of Primal pains—is not valid."[19] (Italics his). Is PT a panacea? Janov enthusiastically claims a 95 percent cure rate. If one listens to testimonials of satisfied customers, one might well be impressed with the glowing claims of emotional healing and the elimination of migraine headaches, ulcers, arthritis, menstrual cramps, and asthma. Janov claims that many dramatic physical changes result form his therapy. "For example," he says, "about one-third of the moderately flat-chested women independently reported that their breasts grew."[20]

The EMDR and PT claims, cures, and cases are exceptions in the field of psychotherapy. However, even the EMDR and PT claims, cures, and cases pale in comparison to the claims made for TheoPhostic counseling. We reiterate, **in all our years of writing and research we have rarely seen such extraordinary claims, cures, and cases as touted by Smith**. TheoPhostic echoes both EMDR and PT in claims, cures, and cases, as well in theory and methodology.

Scientific Proof?

If one were examining TheoPhostic counseling from a scientific perspective, rather than simply believing Smith's say-so claims, cures and cases, one would need to proceed with parameters and requirements of proof. Internationally recognized astronomer Alan Hale restates in an article what all reputable scientists know:

1) Extraordinary claims require extraordinary evidence. . . .
2) The burden of proof is on the positive. If you are making an extraordinary claim, the burden is on

you to produce the extraordinary evidence to prove that you are correct; the burden is not on me to prove that you are wrong.[21]

In all his written material and tapes, we find that Smith has violated both principles. We found no "extraordinary evidence" and no "proof." There is no outside, third-party evidence or support for TheoPhostic theory or methodology. The evidence for the TheoPhostic system's success is essentially Smith's say-so. Subjective, personal testimonials alone do not carry weight as evidence or proof in scientific investigation.

We ask our readers to use the following to evaluate TheoPhostics or any other such system of extravagant claims, cures, and cases:

1. Does it advertise quick cures?
2. Does it guarantee or almost guarantee a quick cure?
3. Does it depend on testimonials?
4. Does it advertise or utilize cases as a means of proof?
5. Does it make extreme claims?
6. Does it provide verifiable, replicable research to back up its claims, cures, and cases?
7. Does it open its doors to third party researchers?

In reference to TheoPhostic counseling, the answers to the above questions would be "yes" for questions one through five and "no" for questions six and seven.

However, none of the above need be considered if God truly revealed the TheoPhostic system to Smith as he claims. If, as we suspect, no outside, third-party research has been done, none would be needed if TheoPhostic truly is a divine revelation from God. Even if objective research were done and it demonstrated that TheoPhostic is no more effective than any other psychotherapy, then that too should be ignored if, indeed, God is the direct source. Even if research were conducted and it showed that TheoPhostic methods produce worse results than all the other psychotherapies, that would not matter either if the true source is God Himself. As a matter of fact, if TheoPhostic is truly divine revelation from God, it should not matter if its use is shown to be detrimental or even harmful at times. And, even if research proved that none of the conversions claimed by Smith were true conversions, it still would not matter. **We suspect , however, that, like the snake oil salesman of old, there is only the unsubstantiated puffery of Smith's claims, cures, and cases, absent any divine revelation or academic proof.**

Notes:

[1] Allen E. Bergin and Sol L. Garfield, eds. *Handbook of Psychotherapy and Behavior Change*, Fourth Edition. New York: John Wiley & Sons, Inc., 1994, p. 824.

[2] Raymond J. Corsini and Alan J. Auerbach, eds. *Concise Encyclopedia of Psychology*, Second Edition, Abridged. New York: John Wiley & Sons, Inc., 1998, p. 133.

[3] *Ibid.*, p. 140.

[4] Francine Shapiro and Margot Silk Forrest. *EMDR: The Breakthrough "Eye Movement" Therapy for Overcoming Anxiety, Stress, and Trauma.* New York: Basic Books, 1997, p. 7.

[5] *Ibid.*, p. 7.

[6] *Ibid.*, p. 11.

[7] *Ibid.*, p. 18.

[8] *Ibid.*, p. 25.

[9] *Ibid.*, p. 29.

[10] *Ibid.*, p. 16.

[11] *Ibid.*, p. 19.

[12] *Ibid.*, p. 241.

[13] *Ibid.*, p. 47.

[14] *Ibid.*, p. 223.

[15] *Ibid.*, pp. 225, 226.

[16] *Ibid.*, p. 228.

[17] *Ibid.*, pp. 229, 230.

[18] *Ibid.*, p. 230.

[19] Arthur Janov, *The Primal Scream*. New York: Dell Publishing Co., Inc., 1970, p. 134.

[20] *Ibid.*, p. 154.

[21] Alan Hale. "An Astronomer's Personal Statement on UFOs," *Skeptical Inquirer*, March/April, 1997, p. 29.

3

Misuse of Scripture in TheoPhostics

We sought Scriptural verification from Smith for his TheoPhostic teachings. After all, if TheoPhostic counseling is truly a divine, latter-day revelation, there should be Scriptural support. After reading every Bible verse used by Smith in the TheoPhostic context, we conclude that any Christian psychotherapist using any particular psychological approach, no matter how contrary it would be to Smith's TheoPhostic approach, could massage the same verses to support what they do.

After reading the TheoPhostic manual and hearing Smith on tape, we attempted to find some clue in Scripture as a prelude to the latter-day, divine revelation Smith claims. We found none. We conclude that the patriarchs and prophets of the Old Testament and the writers of the New Testament were totally ignorant of anything resembling TheoPhostic counseling. If one is to believe Smith, one would have to believe that the Holy Spirit of God revealed something very special to Smith that had never been revealed to any person God used to write the Bible.

Smith claims:

> It [TheoPhostic counseling] is based on the words of
> Jesus who said, "when you know the truth, the truth
> will set you free . . . for when the Son of man sets you
> free, you will be free indeed!"[1]

Such a statement is a not-too-subtle way of equating Scripture (to which Jesus was referring) to what people believe
they hear directly from God during TheoPhostic counseling. This makes sense if one believes that Smith's
TheoPhostic system is indeed a divine, latter-day revelation and that God gives supernatural revelation directly
to the client within the process of TheoPhostic counseling.
Similar patterns and inferences are made throughout
Smith's manual, where Bible verses are quoted as if they
are referring directly to TheoPhostic counseling.

Excursion into Extremities

An example of Smith's excursion into extremities is
found in his use of 2 Corinthians 10:3-5. The following is
his rendition of the verse with his TheoPhostic system
additions in parentheses:

> For the weapons of our warfare (one being
> *TheoPhostic* therapy) are not carnal, but divinely
> powerful through God for the pulling down of strong
> holds (the lies embedded in the memories); Casting
> down imaginations (false thinking), and every high
> thing exalting itself against the knowledge of God
> (logical and reasonable thinking) and bringing into
> captivity (embracing) every thought (stirring up the
> darkness) to the obedience of Christ (hearing the
> truth of God setting the person free) 2 Cor. 10:3-5 (p.
> 194).

One wonders how Christians managed for nearly 2000 years prior to Smith's formulation gleaned from secular psychological theorists. Smith forces these verses to fit his theory and then, just to be sure his readers do not slip into logical or reasonable thinking, he identifies "logical and reasonable thinking" with "every high thing exalting itself against the knowledge of God." However, rather than "logical and reasonable thinking" being among "every high thing exalting itself," as Smith claims, "logical and reasonable thinking" is a gift of God. Without "logical and reasonable thinking," one could not read and understand Scripture. God communicates His Word (the Bible) to people through logical sentences that must be understood by thinking reasonably, not through illogical sentences that are to be understood by thinking unreasonably. One must evidently be committed to illogical and unreasonable thinking to buy into Smith's TheoPhostic system.

Read Smith's rendition of 2 Corinthians 10:3-5 again to see the enormity of the implications involved in what Smith is communicating. He has constrained and distorted Scripture to fit his system, making it conform to such psychological fantasies as a deterministic unconscious filled with forgotten memories that control a client's life and such inner healing techniques as "stirring up the darkness," as well as with the notion that the images and thoughts that come at that point of intense emotional involvement, created by "stirring up the darkness," are God speaking. Thus the very meaning of the verse has been changed by Smith so that the final authority is no longer the Bible itself, but rather the psychological interpreter of Scripture. One has to wonder how many people will now understand 2 Corinthians 10:3-5 through the colored lens of TheoPhostic notions.

Smith likewise inserts his own parenthetical self-serving comments and TheoPhostic applications in his rendition of Ephesians 6:10-18, thus constraining Scrip-

ture to fit his TheoPhostic mold (p. 194). Of course, Smith's
rendition and interpretation of 2 Corinthians 10:3-5 and
Ephesians 6:10-18 fit perfectly with his tale of how God
divinely and directly revealed TheoPhostic counseling to
him, so rapidly that he says, "I could not write down the
new information fast enough to keep up with what **God
was saying to me**" (pp. 164, 165). (Bold added.) Consider
the many so-called latter-day prophets who have claimed
direct revelation from God that came so rapidly that it
was hard to keep pace with it.

No Biblical Evidence
     Smith says:

> When I first saw God apparently heal people in these
> ways and means I ran to the Scriptures to verify these
> methods. **I could not find any biblical evidence**
> which was quite like this. This concerned me until I
> was able to let God out of the box I had Him in. God
> is not and has not limited His works and actions to
> the events of the written Word (p. 111). (Bold added.)

Smith admits no "biblical evidence which was quite like
this." Smith is accurate about that; there is NO biblical
evidence for TheoPhostic. But, if Smith truly received
TheoPhostic from God, as he claims, then no biblical
evidence would be needed, unless, of course, one believes
God would leave the entire New Testament church without such important divine revelation for nearly 2000 years.
     Nonetheless, Smith does **attempt** to use Scripture to
support what he does. Every chapter begins with a Bible
verse. And, there are Bible verses in the text as well. Smith
quotes the following translation of John 14:12: "What I
am saying is the truth, the one that believes on Me, the
works that I do will he do also; and even greater works
than these will he do; because I go unto the Father." It is

no stretch of logic to say that Smith includes what he teaches and does as among those Jesus identified as "greater works" (p. 111). **Smith has, according to himself, received a revelation from God that he calls** *TheoPhostic* **counseling, confesses that what he does is not found in Scripture, but then attempts to use Scripture to support what he does.**

Smith admits, "He [God] will not violate His biblical standards," but then he continues the statement by saying, "but He will act in ways which will stretch you beyond imagination" (p. 111), which leaves the door open to all kinds of extra biblical doctrines and activity. He then quotes Ephesians 3:20 to support that idea: "Unto him that is able to do exceeding abundantly above all that we ask or think, according to the power that worketh in us." He is thus claiming that God is going to "do exceeding abundantly above all that we ask or think" through TheoPhostic counseling. Smith would admit there are other means, but certainly indicates that he believes TheoPhostic counseling is one of them.

An example of how "biblically" Smith deals with subjects begins by him saying:

> According to the Scriptures, negative emotions such as fear, depression, abandonment, shame, hopelessness, worry, anxiety and powerlessness are the result of faulty thinking and misbelief. I see no biblical excuse for a believer to ever embrace such emotions (p. 40).

Smith expands by saying:

> According to the Scriptures, there is no instance in life where these negative emotions are righteously appropriate. For example, the emotion of worry and anxiety are never biblically acceptable in the life of

the believer. The Scripture says in Philippians four *"to be anxious for nothing."* "Nothing" is an all exclusive word. It allows for no exceptions. Then why do we become anxious so easily? Our brains have been falsely programmed to respond to life based on previous experience (p. 40).

Smith's explanation for the existence of these negative emotions does not come from the Bible. It comes from cognitive-behavioral theories and therapies. Thus, he slips nonbiblical dogma into the midst of quoting and interpreting Scripture. Sins of worry and fear are explained and treated psychologically according to Smith's system.

Smith reasons, "But if I can truly embrace the truth 'my God shall supply all my needs according to His riches in glory' there will be no worry or fear present" (p. 40). Since embracing truth is what Smith claims happens in TheoPhostic, this implies that everyone who has fear, worry or anxiety needs TheoPhostic counseling.

Eisegesis

Smith tells the story of Jesus and His disciples in a boat during a storm. Smith quotes Jesus asking His disciples, "How is it that ye have no faith?" after He had calmed the sea and wind. Smith then takes an unwarrented leap away from the clear biblical statement and right into metaphysical speculation when he says:

> Jesus is still willing to speak into the storms of people's lives making everything completely calm. Jesus is still asking each of us the same question, "do you still have no faith?" (p. 41).

The verse has to do with a specific event in the physical world. The Bible is not speaking about emotional storms in people's lives, but rather Jesus' supernatural power over the physical elements. Smith is using the verse to support something the verse says nothing about.

Based on his metaphorical interpretation of Scripture and his erroneous application of Scripture to his counseling system, Smith says, "*TheoPhostic* counseling can make it possible for a person to be relieved totally from all their shame and guilt" (p. 41). There are problems with Smith's reasoning. His comment about Jesus being "willing to speak into the storms of people's lives making everything completely calm" may or may not be universally true. The Scripture he uses does not even apply. Furthermore, Jesus may leave people in their turmoil for a period of time. Many of the prophets and patriarchs were left in their turmoil; the disciples suffered much and some were martyred.

Smith's relating this verse to what he wants to say is known in theology as eisegesis, making the Bible fit a preconceived notion. But, the most egregious part of Smith's reasoning would lead one to conclude that TheoPhostic counseling is used by God to do what Jesus would want done, which, according to Smith, is to relieve persons "totally from all their shame and guilt." There is no such teaching or example in the entire Bible of God doing this through such a system of counseling. Believers are saved, justified, forgiven, and sanctified by grace through faith because of what Jesus did on Calvary, and such gracious acts come through the operation of the Holy Spirit rather than through the techniques of such psychologically-bound systems as TheoPhostic counseling.

At the beginning of each chapter and throughout the TheoPhostic manual there are Bible verses. Read each one and discern what it is that Smith is communicating. Keep in mind that according to Smith, his TheoPhostic system is a latter-day revelation from God. Therefore, it naturally follows that one can freely use Scripture and apply it to whatever he does. A number of verses refer to the light and to the darkness. The implication is that

TheoPhostic counseling is the light and will bring light to those individuals in darkness. We advise that one should read the Bible verses used throughout the manual, think about how they are used, and discern what Smith is communicating regarding his claimed revelation called "*TheoPhostic* counseling."

TheoPhostic Interpretation of Scripture

A volume could be written solely on Smith's misuse of Scripture and his apparent equating of TheoPhostic counseling with what the Scripture teaches and the biblical references to healing. Just a few examples will be given from the numerous ones in the manual in hopes of encouraging others to do an expanded examination of the devious extent to which Scriptures are used.

Smith paraphrases and expands the story of Jesus healing a man lying by the pool of Bethesda (p. 148) as a springboard to introduce his section titled "Basic Principles of Healing" (p. 148). He then imposes his principles onto this brief account in Scripture. His "Principle One" is "Jesus sought out the crippled man, not vice versa." Smith says, "The man was practicing traditional therapy. . . waiting for the water to move. . . looking to the wrong source for help. . . . he was not even looking in the right direction for healing" (p. 149). Smith then makes the following application based on his metaphorical interpretation of the verse rather than a literal interpretation:

> One day, a young lady came to my office who was depressed and filled with hopelessness. She said to me, "I don't even know why I am even here." Jesus had sought her out. Within that session she was healed (p. 149).

One gets the distinct message that this Bible account is not just talking about the man Jesus healed, but is also talking about individuals who become involved in "traditional therapy," which is "the wrong source for help," and who need to look "in the right direction for healing," which in Smith's presentation is none other than TheoPhostic counseling. The example of the lady "depressed and filled with hopelessness" placed in the context of Jesus healing the crippled man gives the impression that this lady fit the description of the crippled man, that she had evidently been "looking to the wrong source" and had not even been "looking in the right direction for healing," until "Jesus had sought her out" and led her right into Smith's supernaturally inspired TheoPhostic system. Not only is Smith proclaiming here that TheoPhostic counseling is the right source and the right direction; Smith is further claiming that Jesus Himself directs people right into his TheoPhostic counseling practice. As he says, "Jesus had sought her out" just as Jesus had sought out the crippled man. Smith clearly teaches that God directly gave him TheoPhostic counseling and **here he is announcing that Jesus supernaturally directs people to TheoPhostic counseling,** just as he came to the crippled man at the pool of Bethesda. And, just as the crippled man was instantly healed, one session of TheoPhostic counseling was enough to heal the lady. Smith declares:

> *TheoPhostic* counseling works because it is divine. Jesus is still healing people and has provided us with a means of accessing His touch. Now it is up to us to use it (p. 151).

As one looks at Smith's other seven principles, the same puffing of TheoPhostic counseling and the same Theo-Phostic-controlled interpretation of Scripture occur.

In a section titled "Personal preparation for the *TheoPhostic* session," Smith says, "The Apostle Paul offers advice for being a prepared *TheoPhostic* counselor in

Ephesians 6" (p. 164). How could the Apostle Paul give "advice for being a prepared *TheoPhostic* counselor" when Smith had not yet invented TheoPhostic counseling, which is heavily dependent on present-day psychological theories? Moreover, if Paul is advising on its use, why did he withhold TheoPhostic counseling from the believers of his day and throughout the next nearly 2000 years?

Smith describes finding "freedom from these painful feelings" through experiencing "healing of the memory" in which the "lie" is exposed. In the midst of re-experiencing the "memory," Smith guides the client to listen for God to speak directly to him. Smith equates what the person then hears and thus receives as "receiving the word implanted which is able to save (heal) their soul" (p. 180). The Scripture having to do with "the word implanted" has nothing to do with the process of TheoPhostic. The verse Smith is quoting or paraphrasing is actually James 1:21. In context it reads:

> Of his own will begat he us with the word of truth, that we should be a kind of firstfruits of his creatures. Wherefore, my beloved brethren, let every man be swift to hear, slow to speak, slow to wrath: For the wrath of man worketh not the righteousness of God. Wherefore lay apart all filthiness and superfluity of naughtiness, and receive with meekness the engrafted word, which is able to save your souls. But be ye doers of the word, and not hearers only, deceiving your own selves (James 1:18-22).

This passages is talking about God's Word as revealed in the Old Testament and to the New Testament apostles and prophets. However, Smith contends that what a client hears under the influence of TheoPhostic is God Himself speaking. Therefore, he makes no apparent distinction between the Bible and what the client hears at the cathartic point of TheoPhostic. Thus, Smith applies James

1:21, which refers to God's written word and the teachings of the New Testament apostles and prophets, to the words the client supposedly hears in the TheoPhostic process. Whether Smith intends to equate what comes into the clients mind with Scripture, one is forced to conclude that both are presented as equal in essence and authority. Smith quotes or paraphrases James 1:21 in such a way as to make it say what it does not say and thereby confuses its intended meaning and application.

Elsewhere he paraphrases the last part of 2 Corinthians 5:17 as "The old indeed is passed away and behold all things have become new" to support his computer brain model in which the old brain program has to be gotten rid of through TheoPhostic before people can access the new computer program (p. 141). The Bible verse has nothing to do with programming the brain as one programs a computer. The verse is speaking about the very nature of the person who is in Christ: "Therefore if any man *be* in Christ, *he is* a new creature: old things are passed away; behold, all things are become new." This is just one more of the many examples of eisegesis in Smith's manual.

Self-Serving Application

Smith quotes Ephesians 6:11-18 and then begins a section titled "Prepare yourself for battle" in which he makes a myopic application to himself and his TheoPhostic counseling. He quotes Ephesians 6:11-13 as follows:

> . . . *Put on the whole armour of God, that ye may be able to stand against the wiles of the devil. For we wrestle not against flesh and blood, but against principalities, against powers, against the rulers of the darkness of this world, against spiritual wickedness in high places. Wherefore take unto you the whole armour of God, that ye may be able to withstand in the evil day. . .* (p. 165).

Smith declares:

> I have never, in all my Christian life and ministry,
> been made so aware of the presence of evil in the
> lives of people. . . . I have never been as harassed by
> the presence of evil as I have since using this method.
> I am constantly being bombarded with thoughts I do
> not wish to think, with pains I did not have before,
> with oppressions I have to pray away (p. 165).

Smith tells about all the satanic harassment that has
happened to him since, according to him, God revealed
TheoPhostic counseling to him and he began using it. The
implication is obvious. Smith is letting his reader know
that what he is doing is directly from God and very important. How? By saying the devil is harassing him. Here
again Scripture is used to support Smith's activities and
his supposed divine revelation. Smith takes Scripture and
then makes applications that may or may not be true, but
few will question his applications, because he makes them
sound biblical. Just because Scripture warns about the
devil and a person is having difficulties does not mean
the person is necessarily doing God's will or striving
against the devil. He may even be striving against the
truth of God that does not fit his preconceived ideas.

In the subsection titled "Know your place of authority
and stand in it with confidence," Smith says, "Position
yourself in the authority of Jesus Christ and stand firm
against the enemy during the session" (p. 166). Such a
statement makes it sound as if the TheoPhostic counselor
is truly doing God's work, based on God's direct revelation, and is therefore able to take divine authority over all
he sees as evil in the session, whether it is evil or not.

If TheoPhostic counseling were truly a divine revelation given directly from God the Father to Smith, then he
might position himself **in** the authority of God's Son. But,

if TheoPhostic counseling is simply Smith's eclectic invention made up of humanistic ideas, but attributed to God, what authority does he have that he does not give to himself? True believers position themselves where they have already been placed, **in** Christ and **under** His authority. They stand against the wiles of the devil by standing **in** Christ actively utilizing all that He has given them in Himself. Jesus had great authority, but even He positioned himself **under** the Father's authority, even when He declared, "All power is given unto me in heaven and in earth" (Matt. 28:18).

Theological Problems

In addition to misapplying and misinterpreting Scripture to support TheoPhostic counseling, Smith makes significant doctrinal statements that have grandiose implications, but without Scriptural support. He says, "Men will usually have more difficulty hearing God's truth than women. Both men and women have more difficulty than children" (p. 56). It is difficult to tell, but one suspects that Smith is referring to TheoPhostic as God's truth regarding women and children hearing God more easily than men. However, Smith does not explain why God used men to write the Scriptures or why most of the prophets and all of the apostles were men rather than women and children.

Smith's theology of sin is also psychologically bound. He defines *sin* as "any choice we make which is less than God's ideal desire for our lives," including "vain attempts to relieve ourselves of our pain" (p. 5). One has to ask how one might know God's ideal desire for one's life in areas of Christian liberty. And, where in Scripture is the attempt to relieve pain necessarily sinful? Smith has taken Freudian defense mechanisms (to be discussed later in this critique) and turned them into sins. In quoting Romans 6:1-2, Smith parenthetically defines *sin* as "the lies of our history," which for Smith are erroneous interpretations of events that occurred during one's childhood (p. 18). This would mean that any misinterpretation of someone else's actions constitutes sin. Where is that in the Bible?

Related to Smith's unbiblical theology of sin is his unbiblical theology of Christian helplessness. In the midst of quoting Romans 7:22-8:2, Smith defines the "law of sin" as "lies" and explains, "In other words I know what to do; it is just that I lack the power to do it. The deception of the lie prohibits me" (p. 137). Thus Smith has interpreted this passage of Scripture according to Freudian psychic determinism. Smith also directs would-be TheoPhostic counselors to "show the client how hopelessly powerless they are to their sin" (p. 186). The reason Smith thinks Christians who are indwelt by Christ are powerless over sin is because he has bought into the Freudian theory of unconscious determinants of behavior, which says that people's actions are the result of powerful unconscious material formed through early-life experiences. Thus for Smith, people sin because of what is in their unconscious rather than because they choose to act in one way or another. This is contrary to Scripture. Were the apostles and early Christians powerless over sin? Paul confidently declared "I can do all things through Christ which strengtheneth me" (Phil. 4:13). "All things" would certainly include resisting sin.

Christians are not only saved from the condemnation of sin; they have new life, and the Holy Spirit enables them to overcome the power of sin. Because Christ provided new life, Paul could say:

> Likewise reckon ye also yourselves to be dead indeed unto sin, but alive unto God through Jesus Christ our Lord. Let not sin therefore reign in your mortal body, that ye should obey it in the lusts thereof. Neither yield ye your members *as* instruments of

unrighteousness unto sin: but yield yourselves unto God, as those that are alive from the dead, and your members *as* instruments of righteousness unto God. For sin shall not have dominion over you: for ye are not under the law, but under grace (Romans 6:11-14).

The Christian is not powerless over sin unless he is walking according to the flesh. Even at that point he is not powerless because he can immediately turn to Christ, confess his sin, be cleansed, and start walking according to the spirit again (1 John 1:9; Romans 8). But, if Christians believe the lie that in Christ they are powerless over sin they are easy prey for all kinds of psychological nonsense.

Charging for Divine Revelation

Smith claims that TheoPhostic counseling is a divine revelation and yet he charges money for it. According to I Corinthians 9:7-14 and other verses, one who ministers can be financially supported, but there is nothing in Scripture that allows the one who ministers to charge a fee. Before Jesus sent His disciples out, he said, "Freely ye have received, freely give." (See Matt. 10:5-10). Jesus' disciples were supported by the people as they ministered from town to town, but can you imagine them charging? Not only is Smith unbiblical to charge for personal ministry, but those who believe this is a divine revelation are also in error to pay for it. They are like Simon the sorcerer in Acts 8.

There is a difference between personal ministry and a ministry of providing material goods. We are not critical of those who charge for tapes, videos, manuals and books, unless the charge is exorbitant. Compare the listed prices of these items from Smith with similar items available elsewhere. Tape for tape, video for video, and workshop for workshop, are the charges for learning TheoPhostic counseling appropriate? After comparing, you decide. Also, you decide whether buying and then selling divine revelation were what Simon the sorcerer had in mind in the Book of Acts.

Misuse of Scripture for Further Analysis

There are numerous additional theological problems with Smith's TheoPhostic teachings. We have decided merely to list a few of them here with some page references from the manual as a source for others who may want to critique his use of Scripture.

> **Wounds versus sins**: pages 182ff, also pages 5 and 47ff.
>
> **God speaking the same to unbelievers as to believers**: page 235.
>
> **Unconditional love**: page 270.
>
> **Mankind as worthy of God's forgiveness**: page 248.
>
> **Generational wounds**: pages 125, 155, 206-207, 267.
>
> **Demonism**: pages 70, 77-78, 119, 165, 194-260 (Chapter 16).

Smith's skewering of Scripture with his TheoPhostic insertions, such as in his rendition of Ephesians 6:10-18 and 2 Corinthians 10:3-5, as well as elsewhere, **should be enough to turn Christians away from this self-proclaimed prophet of God and his psychological eclecticism offered as divine revelation**.

Note:
[1] Ed M. Smith. "Breakthroughs in Biblical Counseling and Genuine Inner Healing." FAX regarding TheoPhostic Training Seminars, Campbellsville, KY, p. 4.

4

Mind
and
Memory

Past and particularly early-life experiences are central in both TheoPhostics and EMDR (Eye Movement Desensitization and Reprocessing). Thus, focusing on memory is a critical element in both systems of therapy. The following quotes from Shapiro and Forrest's book *EMDR* will reveal such dependence on memory:

> One principle that guides the practice of EMDR, outlined in the accelerated information processing model, is that pathologies, or "flaws" of character development, are based on early life experiences. Unless the cause of the problem is organic, or biochemical, everything we feel or do, every action we take, is guided by previous life experiences, because all of them are linked together in an associative memory network.[1]

> Because past and present are connected in our associative memory network on many levels, the

positive treatment effects spread throughout the system, and the person can begin to respond in a positive way to similar situations.[2]

EMDR's ability to open memory networks and process old experiences allows people to emerge from treatment healed beyond their original complaint.[3]

TheoPhostic's complete dependence on memory is seen throughout its teachings as well. The following terms are repeated throughout and represent a sample of the terms used: "traumatic memory," "original memory wound," "original lie in the memory," "lies in the memories," "traumatic memory data," "traumatic memory event," "memory sensation," "total memory experience," "painful memory," "historical memory picture," and "historical memory event." In addition, Smith has other terms connected to his teachings on memory. The following is a small sample of these terms that are repeated throughout his teachings: "unresolved historical moment," "original wound," "original lie," "historical wound," and "former wounds."

The use of memory with its various referents thoroughly saturates TheoPhostic teachings. From the TheoPhostic manual we compiled a list of the uses of memory, regardless of the terminology used. The list extends over a number of pages.

One of the unfortunate problems with Smith is that he speaks authoritatively about the complexities of memory completely without footnotes. His memory pronouncements are extensive and authoritative sounding but not accurate. For example, Smith uses a computer analogy to the mind. In one place he uses "a spread sheet program on a computer" to explain "how a chain or linked lie works" (p. 63). In another place he discusses "true healing" and speaks of "reprogramming of a computer with new software" (p. 140). He speaks of the "old program (lies)" and the "new program (truth)" and describes, in computer terms, what can happen when the "new program (truth)" is loaded on top of the "old program (lies)" (pp. 140, 141). According to Smith all kinds of problems are still possible in this human computer when truth is loaded onto the hard drive while the lies are still stored there. However, Smith assures his readers that "*TheoPhostic* counseling does not load the new program on top of the old" (p. 141).

In a lengthy section titled "The multifaceted soul," Smith uses the computer analogy considerably. He begins by saying:

> The soul is in constant process of gathering, storing, categorizing, and retrieving data as needed by the spirit of the person. This data is stored in compartments which are filed according to category and type. These files are memories encoded in the structure of the brain. Each memory file has many additional subentries such as who was present at the original event, where the event occurred, what happened, the sounds, smells, and other visuals. The mind constantly works receiving and filing information. In this process the soul is not making any interpretation of this data, rather simply gathering and categorizing and filing it according to type (pp. 172, 173).

Smith speaks of how "The brain works according to priority" (p. 174). He says:

> The memories with the pain will take priority due to the *protection factor*. . . . This function of the mind operates like a high speed computer. For those of you who are familiar with a database program on the computer, this analogy will be helpful. A database is made up of records of information categorized according to type. This information is accessed by

entering a particular bit of information causing the program to search throughout all the fields looking for a match (p. 174).

After giving an example of this computer function, Smith says:

> The brain works in the same way. It receives information by way of external stimuli and then takes this information and seeks to associate it with other previously recorded data. When the brain computer finds a match it brings this information to the forefront for the spirit of the person to use to make its next move (p. 174).

In the pages that follow, Smith expands on the brain as a computer analogy and presents some personal opinions as facts, such as the following statement:

> The lie is embedded in the memory banks of the brain while the truth is located in a different part with other logical facts. The person is not able to access both areas at the same time (p. 258).

Contrary to Smith's many assumptions about the brain as computer, Dr. John Searle, in his Reith Lecture "Minds, Brains, and Science," said:

> Because we don't understand the brain very well we're constantly tempted to use the latest technology as a model for trying to understand it.
>
> In my childhood we were always assured that the brain was a telephone switchboard. ("What else could it be?") And I was amused to see that Sherrington, the great British neuroscientist, thought that the brain worked like a telegraph system. Freud often

compared the brain to hydraulic and electro-magnetic systems. Leibniz compared it to a mill, and now, obviously, the metaphor is the digital computer. . . .

The computer is probably no better and no worse as a metaphor for the brain than earlier mechanical metaphors. We learn as much about the brain by saying it's a computer as we do by saying it's a telephone switchboard, a telegraph system, a water pump, or a steam engine.[4]

What Searle is getting at is the fact that the brain is not a mechanical piece of technology. In his book *Remembering and Forgetting: Inquiries into the Nature of Memory*, Edmund Bolles says, "The human brain is the most complicated structure in the known universe."[5] In introducing his book he says:

For several thousand years people have believed that remembering retrieves information stored somewhere in the mind. The metaphors of memory have always been metaphors of storage: We preserve images on wax; we carve them in stone; we write memories as with a pencil on paper; we file memories away; we have photographic memories; we retain facts so firmly they seem held in a steel trap. Each of these images proposes a memory warehouse where the past lies preserved like childhood souvenirs in an attic. This book reports a revolution that has overturned that vision of memory. Remembering is a creative, constructive process. There is no storehouse of information about the past anywhere in our brain.[6]

After discussing the scientific basis for memory and how the brain functions, he says: "The biggest loser in this notion of how memory works is the idea that computer memories and human memories have anything in common." He goes on to say, **"Human and computer memories are as distinct as life and lightning."**[7] (Bold added.)

Medical doctor and researcher Nancy Andreasen says in her book *The Broken Brain* that "there is no accurate model or metaphor to describe how [the brain] works." She concludes that "the human brain is probably too complex to lend itself to any single metaphor."[8]

The current research demonstrates that computer memory and biological memory are significantly different. Unlike a computer, **the memory does not store everything that goes into it**. First, the mind sifts through the multitude of stimuli that enters it during an actual event. Then time, later events, and even later recall color or alter memories. During the creative process of recall, sketchy memories of events may be filled in with imagined details. And, an amazing amount of information is simply forgotten—gone, not just hidden away in some deep cavern of the mind. Memory is neither complete nor fixed. Nor is it accurate. As researcher Dr. Carol Tavris so aptly describes it:

> Memory is, in a word, lousy. It is a traitor at worst, a mischief-maker at best. It gives us vivid recollections of events that could never have happened, and it obscures critical details of events that did.[9]

In his book *Suggestions of Abuse*, Dr. Michael Yapko has a section on the mind as a computer myth. He says:

> Since its initial rise decades ago, the computer has provided the most common metaphor for the workings of memory. Our brains carry out countless functions at remarkable speeds, just like the computer. The analogy holds that the brain represents the hardware of the computer, while our life experiences,

which are reprogrammed into it, represent the software. If you're suffering from psychological problems, then the computer analogy suggests that you need a new "program" for improving your life after you "erase the old tapes" from your earlier (dysfunctional) "programming." The analogy further holds that "the mind is like a computer, accurately recording and storing bits of information and experiences exactly as they were learned and experienced." The analogy further suggests that everything you experience, no matter how briefly, peripherally, or early in your life, is recorded and available to be remembered under proper conditions. Thus you need only to "push the right button" and the data will surface on the "computer screen of your consciousness" in the exact form in which it was originally programmed into your memory.

Unfortunately, the computer as a metaphor for mental functions has only limited usefulness when it comes to the workings of memory. In fact, the metaphor is so inaccurate that, at least as far as memory is concerned, it would probably be best if we simply discontinued its use altogether. Remembering is *not* just a simple process of retrieving what has been stored. The process of forming a memory is *not* simply the recording and storing of events in their entirety as they actually occurred. The phrase to remember is that "memory is reconstructive, not reproductive." Memories are often formed from multiple sources of information and may be modified over time.

Despite the popular misconceptions regarding memory . . . the fact is that memory can be, and often is, an unreliable mechanism prone to a variety of errors.[10]

Yapko refers to a survey he conducted and says that for those:

> . . . who incorrectly believed in the accuracy and completeness of the mind's recording of events, it then follows that whatever someone remembers is inherently true. Furthermore, it leads to the erroneous belief that all experiences can be remembered if only the right conditions can be created. This belief provides a ripe climate for the suggestion of memories in the attempt to facilitate remembering.[11]

Yapko offers the following "Key Points to Remember":

- The comparison of the mind to a computer is an inaccurate one.
- Memory is reconstructive, not reproductive.
- Memory is a process, not an event. It involves the states of sensory registration, organizing the sensory impressions into meaningful information, storage, and retrieval.
- Many factors influence the accuracy of memory, including level of emotional arousal, expectations, motivations, the methods used to retrieve it, and the time elapsed since its formation.
- Memory, like perception, is selective.
- Certainty that a memory is true does not mean it actually is. Nor does the amount of detail provided or the degree of emotionality accompanying its telling.
- Accurate memory for very early childhood experiences (before the age of two or three) is generally unavailable primarily for biological/developmental reasons.
- There is no evidence that "body memories" can be considered accurate or reliable.

- Therapists and researchers have no reliable means to distinguish authentic from false memories.
- "Confirmation bias" leads therapists to look selectively for information that confirms their preexisting beliefs.
- Memories can be rewritten retroactively with newly acquired information.
- Little is known about repression, including how frequently it occurs and why some do and others don't repress memories of trauma.[12]

Shapiro and Forrest say the following:

Fortunately, in EMDR therapy it is not necessary to know whether a memory is historically accurate or not. It is only necessary to reprocess images that are disturbing to the client. The memory may be accurate, or the product of vicarious traumatization, or outright error. Regardless of the validity, the goal is to remove its negative influence on the client.[13]

Smith would probably say amen to that final quote. The huge deficit here is between the conclusion that memories, true or false, nonetheless exert their influence and that it is the therapist's job to deal with this influence regardless of its validity. However, there is no footnote provided in EMDR to substantiate the idea that false memories motivate behavior and that these false images, memories, wounds by whatever name when discovered, discussed, and dissected will help anyone in the long run aside from the immediate effects of a cathartic experience.

Recovered Memories
The TheoPhostic manual and tapes contain numerous cases of individual clients and the application of this

system to their problems. The case of Paula is a good example of the centrality of memory in the TheoPhostic process. Paula had a feeling (or unpleasant emotion). Smith wants to help her to "find a historical event or memory picture which matches what you feel right now" (p. 21). Smith asks her to "focus on the uncomfortable feeling." He says to Paula, "I want you to just focus on the emotion you feel and drift backwards through time" (p. 22). Smith encourages Paula to "let go of the present picture you see and drift backward through time." Smith tells Paula, "there is very likely an old historical event in which you felt just like you feel now." Paula then says she remembers "a terrible time" (p. 22).

The case of Paula is typical of how TheoPhostic proceeds. We have no way of knowing in any of the numerous other cases where TheoPhostic methods are used whether the memory reported is true or false. There is no indication in the cases we read that Smith questions any of the memories. Nor is there any evidence of any attempt on the part of Smith to corroborate the memories.

It is obvious that many of the memories are what are known as recovered memories. These are memories that are not necessarily true but occur as the result of techniques, such as those used in TheoPhostic counseling, to access the unconscious, the "dark room," the "original memory," the "original lie," etc. Even when the memories are known to be true, the details are often questionable.

The following statements from "Recovered Memories: Are They Reliable?"[14] should be kept in mind when evaluating TheoPhostic counseling:

"The use of recovered memories is fraught with problems of potential misapplication." The American Medical Association, Council on Scientific Affairs, *Memories of Childhood Sexual Abuse*, 1994.

"It is not known how to distinguish, with complete accuracy, memories based on true events from those derived from other sources." American Psychiatric Association, Statement on Memories of Sexual Abuse, 1993.

"The available scientific and clinical evidence does not allow accurate, inaccurate, and fabricated memories to be distinguished in the absence of independent corroboration." Australian Psychological Society, *Guidelines Relating to the Reporting of Recovered Memories*, 1994.

"At this point it is impossible, without other corroborative evidence, to distinguish a true memory from a false one." American Psychological Association, *Questions and Answers about Memories of Childhood Abuse*, 1995.

"Psychologists acknowledge that a definite conclusion that a memory is based on objective reality is not possible unless there is incontrovertible corroborating evidence." Canadian Psychological Association, *Position Statement on Adult Recovered Memories of Childhood Sexual Abuse*, 1996.

"Research has shown that over time memory for events can be changed or reinterpreted in such a way as to make the memory more consistent with the person's present knowledge and/or expectations." American Psychological Association, 1995.

An article in the *Calgary Herald* describes the complexities of memory reconstruction very well. It says:

Recently, courts have become embroiled in debates over the validity of amnesia claims, recovered memories, false-memory syndrome and other quirks of the human mind.

We all know the paths long-ago events take in our memories. They fade and we pick up the crayons and colour them in again a little brighter than before and in slightly different hues. The edges unravel and we embroider them anew. Faces blur, events jumble and rearrange themselves, the timbre of voices heard long ago is lost forever and when we try to pin down distant details they dissolve into shimmery pools of doubt.

Remembering is not a simple straightforward act. It is reconstruction, and in that subconscious tearing down and building up, events are altered and scenes subtly shift. Some memories are erased, others created.[15]

Yes, memories can even be created, not from remembering true events, but by implanting imagined events into the mind. In fact, it is possible for implanted and enhanced memories to seem even more vivid than memories of actual past events. Under certain conditions a person's mind is open to suggestion in such a way that illusions of memory can be received, believed, and remembered as true memories. Exploring the past through conversation, counseling, hypnosis, guided imagery, and regressive therapy **is as likely to cause a person to dredge up false information as true accounts of past events**. In a state of heightened suggestibility a person's memory can easily be altered and enhanced.

Sexual Abuse

Someone once said, "Some therapists are obsessed with sex and some with sexual abuse." Smith admits at the beginning of the TheoPhostic manual that "much of the illustrative material of this manual is about people suffering from the wounds of sexual abuse" (p. 6). He mentions that at one time he led an "Adult Survivors of Sexual Abuse Support Group" (p. 30). This preceded what he calls his "revelation from God" of TheoPhostics. Sexual abuse is not only a primary subject dealt with in TheoPhostics, but many of the practices are illustrated with such cases.

In the case of Paula, after drifting backwards, focusing, and looking for the "memory pictures," she says, "I was raped as a young girl" (p. 22). Cases of sexual abuse, trauma, and other earlier life abuses abound in the TheoPhostic manual. In case after case in the manual, we read about memories of sexual abuse occurring "as a young child" (p. 8), "in her childhood" (p. 12), "years earlier" (p. 52), "as a little girl" (p. 66), "when he was a little boy" (p. 131), "at an early age" (p. 154), "as a child" (213), "as a little preschooler" (p. 214), "as a little boy" (p. 242). The preceding are just a few of the many expressions in the manual and tapes.

Dr. Tana Dineen, in her book *Manufacturing Victims*, makes a distinction between authentic victims (those truly abused) and "Fabricated Victims," who are manufactured as a result of reading a book, going to a seminar, or, as often happens, of being in the kind of therapy that relies on the Freudian view of repression, which is a major ego defense mechanism.[16] Early life memory is the cave in which the therapist goes spelunking in order to excavate and examine early life trauma. The idea is that the traumatic memories of childhood abuse have been repressed and are lodged in the unconscious (TheoPhostic "dark room"). According to Freud and his followers this is the cause of adult psychopathology.

Freud's theory that insight and recovery will occur as a result of excavating childhood sexual abuse is flawed and has been exposed by many writers. As a matter of fact, many of Freud's theories are under attack as never before. Therefore those therapies, including TheoPhostic counseling, are equally questionable.

The subtitle of Yapko's book mentioned earlier is *True and False Memories of Childhood Sexual Trauma*. Yapko makes the following two points:

- Therapists may be so sensitive to abuse issues that they see evidence of abuse where none has actually occurred.
- Suggestive therapy procedures can instill false beliefs in clients, including belief of having been abused.[17]

Smith makes the following comments about sexual abuse:

> I have found that no less than 40-60% of all the females that come to me for counseling have at the root of their pain childhood sexual molestation. . . . Typical statistical reports of cases of sexual abuse for women is around 33-38%. This means we have documented about 35% of our female population to be carrying the wound of sexual abuse. . . . My guess is somewhere around 58-70% of all the female population in America have been sexually wounded. Add to this number the people who are carrying other types of wounds such as verbal, emotional and physical abuse, and one can soon see we are surrounded by people in need of a healing touch (p. 20).

Smith obviously belongs with those feminists and others who believe that early life sexual abuse of women is epidemic. Probably the greatest impetus to the search for memories of forgotten sexual abuse and the expanding number of women who have supposedly been sexually abused in early life is the book *The Courage to Heal* by Ellen Bass and Laura Davis, published in 1988.[18] In that book , as well as many others, the definition of sexual abuse was greatly expanded, thereby leading to the usual "33-38%" figure used by Smith. Even Smith's 58-70%, although subscribed to by few, can be expanded to 100% just by expanding the definition of abuse even more, as he readily does. To the question, "What is sexual abuse?" Smith declares, "*Any sexual behavior acted out upon a child by an adult. This would include sexual words, looks, and / or touch. . . . Sexual abuse is not limited to the confines of sexual contact.*" He refers to the "*ghastly wound*" that results "*when an adult (whom a child should have been able to trust) sexually touches the <u>soul</u> of a child in any fashion*" (p. 21), whatever that means.

E. Sue Blume, who subscribes to an expanded percentage of early life sexual abuse for women says the following about incest:

> Must incest involve intercourse? Must incest be overtly genital? Must it involve touch at all? The answer is no. . . . Incest is not necessarily intercourse. In fact, it does not have to involve touch. There are many other ways that the child's space or senses can be sexually violated. Incest can occur through words, sounds, or even exposure of the child to sights or acts that are sexual but do not involve her.[19]

Dr. Elizabeth Loftus and Katherine Ketcham discuss the topic of "Incest is Epidemic" and make the following comment on Blume's book:

> Blume illustrates her discussion with several examples of incestuous abuse: a father hovering outside the bathroom while a child is inside, or barging

into the room without knocking; an older brother coercing his sister to undress; a school bus driver ordering a student to sit with him; an uncle showing pornographic pictures to a four-year-old; a father's jealous possessiveness or suspicion of the young man his daughter dates; a relative's repeated requests to hear the details of an adolescent's sexual experiences. The event itself is not considered as important in determining whether incest occurs as the child's sub-jective experience—the "way" in which she is treated or touched. Thus, sexual abuse can be inferred from the "way" a priest kisses a child good-bye or the "way" a baby-sitter handles a child when bathing her.[20]

Definitions have expanded and so have the percent-ages. To dramatize his percentages, Smith says the following: "I have not found a person who has been molested sexually as a child which did not have some form of sexual difficulty as an adult" (p. 156). As stated earlier, the burden of proof for this statement is on Smith. But, he must provide this proof to outsiders. We wonder how many he has therapized with "sexual difficulty as an adult" who have been led down the primrose path of memory lane to a false memory of child abuse simply because of Smith's expectations and his client's compliance.

The following is another extravagant claim by Smith:

My estimate is around 75% of any local congrega-tion is hurting deeply from early suppressed wounds. I believe 100% of the members of all congregations (this includes pastors) have some element of woundedness. Even the little bruises and scratches produce handicaps in our daily lives and need to be healed. It is really not a question who is wounded but rather to what extent are we all wounded (p. 20).

Using Smith's expanded definition of woundedness and his use of a variety of questionable psychological techniques related to memory, it's easy for him to make such a claim, and then "Presto!" Everybody can be a client for his latter-day, divine revelation of TheoPhostic counseling.

The following is another list of quotations from "Recovered Memories: Are They Reliable?"[21] that should be kept in mind when evaluating such therapies as TheoPhostic:

"At present there are no scientifically valid criteria that would generally permit the reliable differentiation of true recovered memories of sexual abuse from pseudomemories." Michigan Psychological Association, *Recovered Memories of Sexual Abuse: MPS Position Paper*, 1995.

"The AMA considers recovered memories of childhood sexual abuse to be of uncertain authenticity, which should be subject to external verification." American Medical Association, Council on Scientific Affairs, *Memories of Childhood Sexual Abuse*, 1994.

"Psychiatrists are advised to avoid engaging in any 'memory recovery techniques' which are based upon the expectation of past sexual abuse of which the patient has no memory. Such 'memory recovery techniques' may include drug-mediated interviews, hypnosis, regression therapies, guided imagery, 'body memories,' literal dream interpretation and journaling. There is no evidence that the use of consciousness-altering techniques, such as drug-mediated interviews or hypnosis, can reveal or accurately elaborate factual information about any past experiences including childhood sexual abuse. Techniques on regression therapy including 'age regression' and hypnotic regression are of unproven effectiveness." Royal College of Psychiatrists, *Reported Recovered Memories of child Sexual Abuse*, 1997. (UK)

"There is no single set of symptoms which automatically indicates that a person was a victim of childhood abuse. There have been media reports of therapists who state that people (particularly women) with a particular set of problems or symptoms must have been victims of childhood sexual abuse. There is no scientific evidence that supports this conclusion." American Psychological Association, *Questions and Answers about Memories of Childhood Abuse*, 1995.

"Psychologists recognize that there is no constellation of symptoms which is diagnostic of child sexual abuse." Canadian Psychological Association, *Position Statement on Adult Recovered Memories of Childhood Sexual Abuse*, 1996.

"Previous sexual abuse in the absence of memories of these events cannot be diagnosed through a checklist of symptoms." Royal College of Psychiatrists, *Reported Recovered Memories of child Sexual Abuse*, 1997. (UK)

"Most people who were sexually abused as children remember all or part of what happened to them although they may not fully understand or disclose it." American Psychological Association, *Working Group on Investigation of Memories of Child Abuse*, 1996.

"While traumatic memories may be different than ordinary memories, we currently do not have conclusive scientific consensus on this issue." International Society for Traumatic Stress Studies, *Childhood Trauma Remembered: A Report on the Current Scientific Knowledge Base and its Applications*, 1996.

One writer has said, "Repressed memories of sexual abuse and satanic abuse are the favorites among therapists. All the elements of a good soap opera are there—sex, drama and money."[22] All these are evident in TheoPhostic counseling.

Notes:

[1] Francine Shapiro and Margot Silk Forrest. *EMDR: The Breakthrough "Eye Movement" Therapy for Overcoming Anxiety, Stress, and Trauma*. New York: Basic Books, 1997, pp. 65, 66.

[2] *Ibid.*, p. 67.

[3] *Ibid.*, p. 74.

[4] John Searle. "Minds, Brains and Science." *The 1984 Reith Lectures*. London: British Broadcasting Corporation, 1984, pp. 44, 55-56.

[5] Edmund Bolles. *Remembering and Forgetting*. New York: Walker and Company, 1988, p. 139.

[6] *Ibid.*, p. xi.

[7] *Ibid.*, p. 165.

[8] Nancy Andreasen. *The Broken Brain*. New York: Harper and Row, 1984, p. 90.

[9] Carol Tavris, "The Freedom to Change." *Prime Time*, October 1980, p. 28.

[10] Michael D. Yapko. *Suggestions of Abuse: True and False Memories of Childhood Sexual Trauma*. New York: Simon & Schuster, 1994, p. 65.

[11] *Ibid.*, p. 66.

[12] *Ibid.*, p. 91.

[13] Shapiro and Forrest, *op. cit.*, p. 274.

[14] "Recovered Memories: Are They Reliable?" False Memory Syndrome Foundation, 3401 Market Street, Suite 130, Philadelphia, PA 19104-3318.

[15] *Calgary Herald*, Nov. 16, 1998, quoted in *FMS Foundation Newsletter*, Vol. 8, No. 1, 1999.

[16] Tana Dineen. *Manufacturing Victims; What the Psychology Industry Is Doing to People*, Second Edition. Montreal: Robert Davies Multimedia Publishing,1998.

[17] Yapko, *op. cit.*, p. 41.

[18] Ellen Bass and Laura Davis. *The Courage to Heal*. New York; Harper & Row, 1988.

[19] E. Sue Blume. *Secret Survivors: Uncovering Incest and its Aftereffects in Women*. New York: Ballantine Books, 1990.

[20] Elizabeth Loftus and Katherine Ketcham. *The Myth of Repressed Memory: False Memories and Allegations of Sexual Abuse*. New York: St. Martin's Press, 1994, pp. 142,143.

[21] "Recovered Memories: Are They Reliable," *op. cit.*

[22] Gondlof, Lynn quoted by Susan Smith. *Survivor Psychology: The dark side of a mental health mission*. Boca Raton: FL Upton Books 1995, p. 22.

5

Guided Imagery, Visualization, and Hypnosis

Because of the volume of false memories being created in therapy, the American Psychiatric Association has gone on record as saying, "Memories also can be significantly influenced by a trusted person."[1] It has been known for some time that clients tend to produce material in memory, imagination, free association, and dreams according to their therapist's theories and expectations. Psychoanalytic patients free associate in Freudian ways and analytic patients free associate in Jungian ways. It seems axiomatic that TheoPhostic clients will also produce material (memories) according to the theory and expectations of Smith and others who believe and practice as he does. Nevertheless, Smith denies guiding or directing the client:

> *TheoPhostic* counseling does not need or allow the counselor to guide anything. This process is God directed. Anytime the counselor seeks to direct or guide what is happening in the mind of the person, what they do ceases to be *TheoPhostic* counseling (p. 112).

Dr. Carl Rogers, one of the best-known and most admired humanistic psychologists of the twentieth century, spent a lifetime studying human behavior. He developed a technique of treatment called "nondirective" or "client-centered" therapy, which he believed to be nondirective in that the therapist does not lead the client's attention to any topic or material. The client chooses. It is client-centered in that it proposes to allow the client to have his own insights and make his own interpretations, rather than depend on the therapist to provide the insights and interpretations.

Carl Rogers, in his nondirective therapy, claims that he does not influence the client in any way. Because the person expresses himself any way he chooses, many believe nondirective therapy is truly nondirective. However, Jay Haley says:

> Actually nondirective therapy is a misnomer. To state that any communication between two people can be nondirective is to state an impossibility.[2]

Without intending to do so, a counselor will communicate some response and thus influence the client's thoughts, words, and actions. Two independent studies, conducted ten years apart, showed that Rogers himself was, in fact, a directive counselor. His response to his clients rewarded and punished and therefore reinforced or extinguished their expressions. If Rogers cannot be nondirective, it is certainly unlikely that any other psychotherapist or counselor can refrain from being directive in one way or another. The therapist's expectations and values will seep through any system and influence clients.

To put Smith's assertion of not being directive to the test, one can examine all sentences that contain the first person pronoun ("I") referring to Smith. Notice what is said in each of those sentences and look at the verbs he uses. Add to these the out and out directives used by Smith and one must conclude that, contrary to what he says, Smith is directive. The following are just a few of the numerous examples:

I asked her to imagine herself . . . (p. 43).

I lead him to locate . . . (p. 44).

I ask him to drift back . . . (p. 45).

I asked her to close her eyes and focus . . . (p. 52).

I asked her to disconnect from the picture . . . (p. 52).

Focus on that scared feeling . . . (p. 57).

Focus on that thought . . . (p. 58).

I want you to listen for a truth . . . (p. 58).

I had him access an early memory . . . (p. 63).

Move on to the next memory . . . (p. 64).

I had her "feel" around in the memory . . . (p. 66).

I have them focus on the confusion . . . (p. 70).

I have the client tell themselves how confusing this is . . . (p. 70).

Focus on this hurt . . . (p. 73).

Let him [Jesus] place His hand on your chest (p. 73).

I ask them to sense the presence of Jesus and listen (p. 77).

Tell yourself how shameful you are . . . (p. 77).

I encourage them to speak whatever they hear . . . (p. 77).

We have six additional pages of excerpts from Smith's directive sentences that we could insert here for further proof.

In the above statements and in numerous similar sentences, Smith repetitiously uses such verbs as "think," "feel," "listen," "stir," "drift," "walk," "visualize," and "watch." One must therefore conclude that Smith is directive—very directive. These verbs are stated in what grammarians call the "imperative mood," which is used to make a request, give a command, or give directions. Simply reading what Smith has written clearly demonstrates that TheoPhostic counseling is very directive. It must also be remembered that Smith is in the usual professional therapist's role and is therefore regarded as an expert by his clients. Thus, even his questions and suggestions can be regarded as being directive.

To put Smith's statement about the TheoPhostic counselor not directing or guiding the process to the test, one needs only to examine the client cases as described in the TheoPhostic manual and read the interchanges between Smith and his clients to see just how directive he is. Any impartial evaluation of Smith's work will reveal that he is very directive. Read any page of the manual where a case is presented or an activity described and you will see how directive TheoPhostic counseling really is. For example, we turned to the manual where Smith describes a very important component of TheoPhostic counseling called "Stirring up the darkness." Smith says:

Now I encourage them to immerse themselves deeply into the painful memory and tell themselves the lies which are causing so much pain (p. 107).

Since they are already embracing and confessing the lie I simply intensify their efforts by stirring it up (p. 108).

I have them focus on the picture, tell themselves the lie(s) in the most convincing manner they can, allowing the intense emotions to surface. I will often join in the "stirring" by saying things like, "feel how dirty you are for . . ." "feel the pain and terror of knowing you cannot get away . . ." "feel how guilty you are for letting Him . . ." (p. 108).

If at first they do not hear God speak, ask them to refocus on the event and the lies. Ask them if there [are] any new thoughts which give clearer focus about the lie. Ask if they feel compelled to move to a different memory or lie (p. 108).

Guided Imagery, Visualization, and Hypnosis

Though he would deny it, Smith is guilty of using guided imagery, visualization, and hypnosis. Because early life abuse, particularly sexual abuse, is such a predominant subject in TheoPhostic counseling, we looked at several reference works on this subject and particularly examined how guided imagery, visualization, and hypnosis are related to abuse therapy. Memory is central to all of this. One of the well-known texts is by Dr. Michael Yapko and is titled *Suggestions of Abuse: True and False Memories of Sexual Trauma.* Yapko, like Smith, is a psychotherapist, but one who uses his own as well as others' academic research on the subject of abuse and the use of memories.

The content of Yapko's book is well documented with references to research while Smith's is not.

Yapko has indicated ways therapists can suggest abuse. He says, "perhaps the most common and effective technique of all involves first encouraging uncertainty and then providing biased information as though it were objectively true."[3] He gives several steps the therapist uses for eventually suggesting abuse and then says:

> The next step is to do hypnosis, guided imagery, guided meditations, or visualization exercises (or an equivalent process that may go under a different name). The therapist asks suggestive questions, such as: "Who are you with? What is he doing to you? Do you sense he has an erection? Where is he touching you? Don't you feel dirty and used? What is that look on his face telling you?" Up come images of abuse— surprise!—right in line with the theories the therapist has presented as fact. The client emerges from these imagery sessions armed with more and more suggested or confabulated details that seem to further "prove" that abuse must have occurred. The power to misinform and to establish a chain of subsequent reactions is potentially the most dangerous part of any therapy process.[4]

Read again the "suggestive questions" that Yapko lists above. Then read any one of Smith's cases and note the similarity. Yapko's suggested questions and more can be found in some form in Smith's client cases.

In *A Concise Dictionary of Cults and Religions*, William Watson defines guided imagery and visualization interchangeably:

Guided Imagery; also called visualization. Involves relaxation techniques, self-hypnosis, and meditation. The person concentrates on an image in his mind in an effort to make something happen. The image may be suggested by a therapist.[5]

Smith asks his clients to look for Jesus in the picture. He further asks questions about what Jesus is doing and saying.

Dave Hunt says in his book *Occult Invasion*:

Occultism has always involved three techniques for changing and creating reality: thinking, speaking, and visualizing. . . .

The third technique [visualizing] is the most powerful. It is the fastest way to enter the world of the occult and to pick up a spirit guide. Shamans have used it for thousands of years. It was taught to Carl Jung by spirit beings, and through him influenced humanistic and transpersonal psychology. It was taught to Napoleon Hill by the spirits that began to guide him. Agnes Sanford . . . was the first to bring it into the church. Norman Vincent Peale was not far behind her, and his influence was much greater. . . .

Visualization has become an important tool among evangelicals as well—which doesn't purge it of its occult power. Yonggi Cho has made it the center of his teaching. In fact, he declares that no one can have faith unless he visualizes that for which he is praying. Yet the Bible states that faith is "the evidence of things not seen" (Hebrews 11:1). Thus visualization, the attempt to "see" the answer to one's prayer, would work *against* faith rather than help it! Yet Norman Vincent Peale declared, "If a person consciously visualizes being with Jesus that is the best guarantee I know for keeping the faith" . . . .

Of Christ, Peter said, "Whom having not seen, ye love; in whom, though now ye see him not, yet believing, ye rejoice with joy unspeakable and full of glory" (1 Peter 1:8). In the previous verse he refers to a future "appearing of Jesus Christ." John likewise speaks of "when he shall appear" (1 John 3:2), and Paul speaks of loving "his [future] appearing" (2 Timothy 4:8). Visualizing Jesus would seem to be an unbiblical attempt to have Him appear before the proper time—unless, of course, one insists that it is only imagination. Yet those who are involved attribute results to this process that could scarcely be explained as resulting from fantasy conversations with oneself.

Furthermore, a "Christ" who would take on any color of hair or eyes and any form to suit the visualizer is not the real Lord Jesus of the Bible and history. Then who is this entity that appears in response to this occult technique to deceive Christians?[6]

Alan Morrison's book titled *The Serpent and the Cross: Religious Corruption in an Evil Age* includes a chapter titled "Sorcerous Apprentices: The Mind-Sciences in the Church Today," which should be read by all who are interested in TheoPhostic counseling. A subsection in that chapter is titled "In Your Mind's Eye: The Occult Art of Visualization" and is a must-read for those who want to learn about the roots and promoters of visualization in the church. The following quotations are from that section:

Fundamental to our study is the fact that the development of the imagination through "visualization" exercises is one of the most ancient and widely used occult techniques for expanding the mind and opening up the psyche to new (and forbidden) areas of consciousness.[7]

The practice of visualization can be used in a variety of ways, but they all fall into three main types. **Firstly**, they can be used to provide a doorway into what psychologists call a "non-ordinary state of consciousness." **Secondly**, they can be used as a means towards something called "Inner Healing" or "Healing of the Memories." **Thirdly**, they can provide an instrument for the manipulation and recreation of matter and consciousness.[8]

Most of the people being seduced into the practice of visualization—especially those within the Church—have not the faintest conception of the occultic aim which lies at its root. In spite of the attractions and harmless benefits put forward by its advocates, visualization is a primary gateway for demonic infiltration into human consciousness—a deception currently being worked on a truly grand scale.[9]

This confusion of an *imagined* Jesus with the *actual* Person of Christ is the fatal flaw in the entire psychotherapeutic visualization process, about which we shall say more shortly. How convenient it is to invite the Jesus of your own imaginings into scenes where sins can be forgiven without repentance—not only those of others who have wronged you, but also your own![10]

A further question can here be raised: if each of these visualized "christs" is *not* the objective, risen Christ of Scripture, then who or what are the entities which are conjured up in the imaginations of professing Christians and others who are encouraged to fantasize these images by Christian psychotherapists? The plain truth is that they are little different to those "inner guides" of the secular visualizer.[11]

What, therefore, should be the response of the Christian to the use of visualizations involving the image of Jesus Christ? Of primary concern should be the fact that this type of activity is specifically forbidden and warned against within the pages of the Bible. It is a solemn fact that every figurative representation of God contradicts His being; and although we do not wish to obscure the fact that Jesus (as God manifested in the flesh) was a real human being, **the conjuring up of a visualized image of Christ for the purposes of mental manipulation is surely a gross form of idolatry.** The last thing that the Christian should be doing is relying on such images in the imagination for guidance in life or to increase faith.[12] (Bold added.)

Guided Imagery and Visualization

Smith says, "*TheoPhostic counseling is not guided imagery*, although visualization plays a great part in the process for some people. Guided imagery is visualization created and guided *by the therapist*" (p. 15). To make the point stronger yet, Smith says:

> *TheoPhostic* counseling is **not** guided imagery, but rather divine guided revelation. The pictures and images people see are not suggestions made by the therapist. . . . When I am working with a person I do not suggest to them what they should see or not see. I simply ask them to watch and listen. Jesus himself will often appear and speak words of healing in the person's mind (p. 15).

Later in the manual, Smith declares, "***TheoPhostic counseling is not in any shape or form guided imagery***" (p. 112).

We have already shown that, contrary to what Smith claims about being nondirective, TheoPhostic counseling, as illustrated by his examples and statements, is directive. We will now demonstrate that, contrary to what Smith claims, he is involved in guided imagery and visualization.

In reading statements quoted from the TheoPhostic manual, one needs to keep in mind that expectation is a powerful force in the therapist-client relationship. Smith expects to work with images related to memories, and the client soon learns to expect likewise. This happens in each therapeutic approach. That is why Freudian clients produce Freudian material and respond in Freudian ways. The therapist is regarded as the expert and the client is there to receive and will therefore respond according to the theories and expectations of the so-called expert. This is further reinforced by the client paying the professional's fees. This is a strong force to conform to TheoPhostic expectations placed on the client by the professional "expert therapist."

Smith writes about the case of a woman named Paula, who was familiar with TheoPhostic counseling because of having attended one of Smith's workshops. She therefore knew how to act and respond as an ideal client in TheoPhostic counseling. Smith asks, "Paula, do you have a *memory picture* that matches the feeling that you experienced tonight?" (p. 21). Please note the words "memory picture." A memory picture is, of course, an image. Paula expresses uncertainty and Smith responds, "It is very probable you have an early childhood event which felt the way you are feeling now. The unpleasant emotions you are experiencing right now are coming from this earlier picture""(p. 21). Smith first says, "very probably," and then becomes more declarative by saying that the emotions "are coming," thereby moving from suggesting a probability to stating a certainty within the space of two sentences.

Nevertheless, Paula says that she can't think of anything like what he is suggesting.

Next Smith directs her thus: "Allow yourself to feel the emotion you were feeling during the workshop earlier." After assuring her that she is "safe here," Smith says that the emotion "is most likely coming from some earlier memory when something terrible must have happened to you." He continues, "What I want to help you do is find a historical event or memory picture which matches what you feel right now" (p. 21). Next he instructs her to close her eyes and "focus on the uncomfortable feeling." He says, "I want you to just focus on the emotion you feel and drift backwards though time" (p. 22).

Smith's next statement is typical of how he guides clients. He says:

> Now that you are focused on the emotions let go of the present picture you see and drift backward through time. Stay focused on the emotions you feel and allow your mind to find the memory which matches the feeling you are presently focused upon. There is very likely an old historical event in which you felt just like you feel now. You do not need to look for the memory, your mind will know when and where to stop. You focus on the feeling (p. 22).

After several interchanges related to the memory picture, Smith says:

> I want you to hear what God has to say to you about these lies. He has a special truth for you. What I need you to do is become very focused on the rape scene (p. 23).

Following another interchange, Smith says:

After the memory and the thoughts become very intense I want you to listen for God to speak to you. I do not want you to make up what you think He might say, just merely listen for His words. Your main responsibility is to stir up the pain and shame of the memory and focus on it (p. 23).

Paula focuses on it and then Smith says, "let the memory become very focused and tell yourself the statements" (p. 23).

There is no question that Smith is orchestrating the session. He is directive and very prescribed in what he does and expects. He guides the client from present emotion to an earlier memory picture (image) and then asks questions and gives directions about the memory picture (image) and the emotions. It is Smith who directs Paula to "focus on the feeling," to "find a historical event or memory," to "hear what God has to say," and to "listen for God."

With the focus on feelings and emotions and the expectation of a memory picture (image) on the part of both the TheoPhostic counselor and the client, it is no wonder that there is so much imagery involved in this type of counseling. This is easily compounded by the fact that some individuals have very fertile imaginations, which would give them more "fantastic" imagery.

Smith uses terms such as "historic memory" and "original memory." Regardless of what memory words are used or their equivalents, one is dealing with an image in the mind. There is a huge difference between an existent or naturally occurring memory (image) of which a person is aware and a memory (image) that is being sought to match a current feeling, emotion, or disturbance. When one compounds a memory (image) that occurs through active hunting and pursuing with animated interchanges that result in personal revelations such as Smith describes, one is truly treading on the dangerous ground of occult activity, regardless of whether one imagines seeing the image of Jesus or God in the process or if one imagines hearing God's words in one's mind as a result.

Central to Smith's therapy is the expectation and encouragement to find Jesus in the memory (image). In his section titled "Finding Jesus in the memory," Smith often reminds the client that Jesus is present. Then, after using his "stirring up the darkness" techniques, he asks them to "look for the presence of Jesus." He says, "If a person cannot visually see Jesus in the memory, I ask them to sense His presence. I ask them to look for the presence of his character; his love, understanding, compassion, and gentleness" (p. 112). Smith says:

> God does not reveal His truth in the same way with every person. He seems to tailor-make it for the individual. He may speak immediately with long flowing phrases or with a single word. Sometimes He speaks with pictures or images. He seems to speak in such a way which is right and characteristic of the person who is seeking His healing. I have even heard God say humorous things to people which immediately lifted their spirits and revealed His wonderful sense of humor (p. 110).

Smith encourages the client to find Jesus in the memory picture and encourages interaction with Him. Read every sentence and every paragraph in which Jesus or God is mentioned to see how Smith functions and how his words and expectations are used to influence the client's imagery.

To avoid quoting a long litany of interchanges and descriptions from the manual, we will give excerpts to save time and space. The quotes are, of course, out-of-context. However, reading them in context would even further demonstrate how important guided imagery and visualization are to TheoPhostic counseling and how deep the dependence on the use of God and Jesus images in the process. Note the imperative verbs used, such as "locate," "see," "sense," "ask," "look, "let," and "drift." These verbs are all related to imagery and movement from one image to another.

As you read excerpts from the manual, notice whether guided imagery/visualization is occurring. Smith says:

> I sometimes create a memory facsimile from the sense of what happened that matches the lie, rather than spend more time digging around for more visual information which I may or may not ever locate (p. 43).

Smith immediately declares, "No, I am not creating a false memory" (p. 43). Is a "memory facsimile" that he is creating a true memory? If it is created by him, it is definitely a created memory with more possibilities for being a false memory than a true memory. Labeling a created memory a "facsimile" does not prevent it from being a false memory. But, even if he is "not creating a false memory," Smith is guiding the client to create a memory that may or may not be true.

Smith encourages clients to use their imagination while they are trying to match their emotions with a forgotten past event. In describing the way he helps people remember, Smith says:

> I asked her if she had any memories which matched that statement and feeling of worthlessness. . . . I asked her to imagine herself being surrounded by her family and hearing them condemn, shame and belittle her (which they often did) (pp. 43, 44).

Suggesting that the client "imagine herself being surrounded by her family," compounded by the expectation of the imagery that is connected to the reported emotion, is certainly a form of guidance. He definitely directs the memory production, specifies details about the thoughts of unnamed individuals, and does his part to intensify the client's emotions in his attempt to get the person to hear the truth from God:

> Focus on that man laying on top of you forcing his penis into your little vagina. Remember the pain and the shame. Think about what others must have thought about you having sex with your abuser. Think about what they thought about you for allowing it to happen. Feel how shameful it is to do this knowing others are aware of your shameful behavior. Feel the guilt, shame, disgust. Let the shame and pain grow as intense as you can possibly stand (p. 84).

One does have to wonder how it is that such a production of the imagination (his and/or his client's) can be the pathway to hearing God's truth.

Smith confesses:

> I will often join in the stirring . . . I ask them to let the emotion stir up as intently as they can stand and wait for God to speak His truth to them" (p. 108).

Smith guides his clients to visualize sex acts and to tell themselves how dirty they feel. He tells a client: "Visualize your husband touching you sexually. Tell yourself how shameful you are for letting him do this. . . . See your father having intercourse with you. Tell yourself how bad you are. . . . See your husband having intercourse with you. . . (p. 257).

Smith repeatedly demonstrates his own expectation that God or Jesus will speak or appear or at least be sensed, that God will reveal His truth directly to the client, and that God reveals Himself and His truth in a variety of ways. Because this is an integral part of Smith's therapeutic system, he naturally expects the client to find, hear, and interact with the image of God or Jesus.

The following are just a few of many examples of how Smith guides the imagery and visualizations involving God and Jesus. Smith says:

> As they are focused on the pain we have them locate Jesus in their mind. When they see Him or at least sense His presence, we ask them to take their hurt and deep pain to Him. We ask them what they see or sense Him doing (p. 72).

> Now look around in your mental picture and look for Jesus. If you do not see Him at least sense His presence . . . Let Him place His hand on your chest. . . After a few moments I ask them to drift back to the memory which feels like this hurt (p. 73).

> I ask the person to tell me where Jesus is and what He is doing. . . . I asked them to listen to Jesus. . . . I asked them to watch Him and see if he does anything. . . . I ask them to report whatever they see Him do. . . . I ask them to feel His love, compassion, tenderness, understanding and comfort (p. 114).

> Try to find Jesus in the picture. He is there somewhere (p. 15).

> I then ask them to search out the picture . . . I will usually ask them to watch Jesus and follow Him (p. 120).

I ask the Lord to make Himself very real to them. I often ask Him to hold them in his arms and show His great love for them. I ask Him to carry them from the room to their place in life and to reassure them of His constant presence in their life (p. 122).

That is all right. Go ahead and hit God. . . . Can you allow Him to hold you? If you can let Him and see how the picture changes (p. 168).

Once it is all stirred up, I have them disconnect momentarily, and look around in the memory picture for Jesus. If they do not see Him, I ask them to try to feel His presence. . . . I have them look over at Jesus. I ask them to tell me what He is doing (p. 187).

I asked her to allow God to speak to her His truth about this picture (p. 241).

I asked him to find Jesus in the picture. . . . I asked him to let Jesus come over to him and hold him (p. 254).

I asked the client to watch Jesus and describe what He is doing. . . . I told the client to follow and see where He would lead him. . . . I asked the person to watch Jesus and see what He would do next. . . . I then instruct the person to follow Jesus to the next memory (p. 258).
I have them follow Jesus to the next memory. . . locate Jesus in this memory. . . . What is He doing? . . . Look at Jesus again and focus on Him (p. 259).

Look at Him and listen. . . . Look over at Jesus and see if He leads you to another memory. . . . Now look over at Jesus and listen to Him. . . . Look over at

Jesus and let him lead you to any other memory. . .
(p. 260).

Follow Jesus again and see where He leads you. . . .
Look over at Jesus and follow him to see if there are
any other memories to be healed (p. 261).

I took her through the *"Follow the leader"* process
letting Jesus lead her through several memories (p.
272).

Smith discusses whether or not the image of Jesus is
the real Jesus or "a fabrication of these people's minds
helping them to concentrate." Smith concludes that he "was
convinced it was the real Jesus." He declares, "I am
convinced Jesus manifests Himself into the mind of the
people and speaks to them directly and in truth" (p. 255).
    Smith gives three ways to test the image to make sure
it is the real Jesus and not a demon. First one must "feel"
Jesus emotionally. The image must "feel loving, compassionate, forgiving, etc." A second test is to look at the
image's face. Smith says, "Satan cannot imitate the face
of Jesus" (p. 212). The third criteria is based on what the
image says. Smith says, "If he speaks words of condemnation, scorn, rejection I know it is an evil spirit" (p. 212).
Smith teaches these three criteria to both clients and
prospective counselors. The bottom line is that if the image
and the words meet Smith's criteria, then the image must
be the real Jesus and the words must be the words of the
real Jesus.
    We wonder if the money changers in the temple and
the Pharisees of Jesus' time were alive today and were
being counseled the TheoPhostic way, what they would
"feel" from their image of Jesus, what the visualized image
of Jesus would look like to them, and what the Jesus image
would say to them. Unlike those currently visualizing

Jesus through TheoPhostic techniques at least they would know what Jesus looked like. The facts are that Jesus at times gave corrections to persons that didn't "feel loving, compassionate, forgiving, etc." at the time, but nonetheless were (e.g., rich young ruler); no one today knows specifically what Jesus looked like; and no know knows exactly what Jesus would say in a specific situation as presented by Smith's clients.

In several places Smith offers what he considers to be proof positive about the visualization experiences of TheoPhostic clients, and that is the commonality of the experience. The commonality has to do with many of the clients having the same experience. In one section of the manual he answers the question, "Is there any significance to the similar repeating images which different people experience?" (p. 262). Smith answers:

> The image which seems to surface the most with different people is what I have come to call the meadow scene. . . . This imagery of the meadow scene has helped me to realize this image of Jesus is not the person's fabrication. Why does this specific scene come into the minds of so many different people unless the same Jesus is producing it (pp. 262, 263).

Smith may not be aware that commonality of experiences occur in occult visualizations, near-death experiences, and through many of the Eastern meditation experiences. **Commonality of experience does not establish the validity or the source of that experience.** The fact that a Jesus is visualized in a meadow by many clients is no proof it is the real Jesus.

Smith believes it inappropriate for the client to ask Jesus "about future events or personal issues" (p. 113). He warns, "To do this is to run the risk of hearing 'deceptive spirits' and misleading your client" (p. 113). Yet, as discussed earlier, Smith tells how to make sure one is visualizing Jesus rather than a demon spirit (pp. 212, 253). Therefore, if one can tell it's the real Jesus, why not ask "about future events or personal issues"?

Hypnosis

Hypnosis has been used as a method of mental, emotional, behavioral, and physical healing for hundreds and even thousands of years.[13] Witchdoctors, Sufi practitioners, shamans, Hindus, Buddhists, and yogis have practiced hypnosis, and now medical doctors, dentists, psychotherapists, and others have joined them. From witchdoctors to medical doctors and from past to present, the rituals and results have been reproduced, revised, and repeated.

The hypnotic trance begins by focusing a person's attention and produces many results. According to its advocates, the practice of hypnotism may alter behavior in such a way as to change habits; stimulate the mind to recall forgotten events and information; enable a person to overcome shyness, fears, and depression; cure maladies such as asthma and hay fever; improve a person's sex life; and remove pain.[14]

Fantastic claims and the increasing popularity of hypnosis in the secular world have influenced many in the church to turn to hypnotism for help. Various Christian medical doctors, dentists, psychiatrists, psychologists and counselors are using hypnosis in their practices and recommending it to Christians.

Christians who support the use of hypnosis do so for some of the same reasons that medical doctors and psychotherapists recommend it. These Christians believe that when hypnosis is practiced by a qualified professional, it is scientific rather than occultic. They distinguish between those who practice it for helpful purposes and those who use it with evil intent. They believe that, although hypnotism can be dangerous in the hands of malevolent individuals or novices, it is a safe and useful tool in the hands of professionally trained, benevolent individuals. They also believe it is safe because they think of hypnosis as an extension of natural, everyday experiences. Finally they contend that a person's will is not violated during the hypnotic trance.

Yapko describes a hypnotic procedure that sounds like what happens in TheoPhostic counseling:

> "Age regression" is a hypnotic procedure in which the client is immersed in the experience of memory. The client may be encouraged to *remember* events in vivid detail, a procedure called "hypermnesia." Or, the client may be encouraged to *relive* the events of the past as if they were going on right now, a procedure called "revivification." Either or both of these procedures are commonly used in memory recovery-oriented therapies.[15]

The American Medical Association, Council on Scientific Affairs, has said:

> The Council finds that recollections obtained during hypnosis can involve confabulations and pseudo-memories and not only fail to be more accurate, but actually appear to be less reliable than nonhypnotic recall.[16]

The suggestions, the emotions, and the focus on feelings in the past rarely produce true memories. In various forms of regressive therapy the therapist attempts to convince the client that present problems are from past hurtful events and then proceeds to help the client remember and re-experience hurtful events in the past. However, rather than positive change, many false memories are produced. Some writers, such as Campbell

Perry, indicate that **such techniques as the eliciting of memories, relaxation, and regression work are often disguised forms of hypnosis.**[17] The leading questions, direct guidance, and voice intonation are enough to serve as an induction into the trance state for many individuals. Mark Pendergrast says:

> The "guided imagery" exercises that trauma therapists employ to gain access to buried memories can be enormously convincing, whether we choose to call the process hypnosis or not. When someone is relaxed, willing to suspend critical judgment, engage in fantasy, and place ultimate faith in an authority figure using ritualistic methods, deceptive scenes from the past can easily be induced.[18]

In his book *Victims of Memory*, Pendergrast quotes several well-known authorities in the field of hypnosis:

> [Martin] Orne asserts that hypnosis is a technique that "greatly facilitates the reconstruction of history, that allows an individual to be influenced unwittingly, and that may catalyze beliefs into 'memories.'" He emphasizes that "we cannot distinguish between veridical [true] recall and pseudomemories elicited during hypnosis without prior knowledge or truly independent proof." [Elizabeth] Loftus has said virtually the same thing. "There's no way even the most sophisticated hypnotist can tell the difference between a memory that is real and one that's created. If you've got a person who is hypnotized and highly suggestible and false information is implanted in his mind, it may get imbedded even more strongly."[19]

Jean-Roch Laurence and Campbell Perry assert: "Hypnosis is a situation in which an individual is asked to set aside critical judgment, without abandoning it completely, and is asked also to indulge in make-believe and fantasy."[20]

Psychiatrist Herbert Spiegel says it more directly: "A good hypnotic subject will vomit up just what the therapist wants to hear."[21]

"It is incredible," wrote French psychologist Hippolyte Berheim in 1888, "with what acumen certain hypnotized subjects detect, as it were, the idea which they ought to carry into execution. One word, one gesture, one intonation puts them on track." Simply urging "Go on" at a crucial point, or asking "How does that feel to you?" can cue the desired response. A person who *agrees* to play the role of the hypnotized subject is obviously motivated to believe in that role and act it properly.[22]

In his TheoPhostic manual, Smith admits, "I can hypnotize a person" (p. 219). While Smith would deny he ever hypnotizes anyone through TheoPhostic counseling, there is no question that there is a great possibility that it occurs. As in hypnosis, Smith's clients are asked to set aside logical, critical thinking. The following are just a few of the many directions given by Smith that could result in a trance state:

I would like for you to close your eyes and focus on the uncomfortable feeling you experienced during today's workshop (p. 22)..

Connie, let you mind be clear of all thoughts and pictures. Simply listen and speak whatever thoughts you hear (p. 143).

I ask the person to close their eyes and focus on the emotion they feel (p. 252).

I begin by placing the person in one of their memories. . . . I have them focus on the memory and "feel" around to see if there are any uncomfortable emotions . . . . Once the memory is clear I ask them to find Jesus in the picture and focus on Him (p. 258).

In surveying "Therapists' Attitudes about Distinguishing False from True Memories," Yapko asked, "Do you attempt to distinguish between what appear to you to be true memories and false memories?"[23] Yapko reports, "Most therapists surveyed admitted they do nothing to differentiate truth from fiction in their clients' narratives."[24]

Thus far we have demonstrated that Smith encourages and expects imagery and visualization. His role as therapist and expert is a powerful force in the relationship which results in a self-fulfilling prophecy, where expectations shape results. At his encouragement, Smith's clients do connect their current pain with past (usually early life) memories (images) and Smith does guide the process. The similarities between what Smith does and occult visualization are obvious. In TheoPhostic counseling there is great danger of being involved in the occult in spite of the claim that the visualized image is Jesus. It also appears axiomatic that some of Smith's clients will fall into a hypnotic trance as a result of the procedures he uses.

Regardless of Smith's fantastic claims, rarely heard in the field of psychotherapy, he has produced no footnotes to support what he says and has provided no academic research by outside, third parties. His phenomenal claims lack the necessary phenomenal proof and seem to depend entirely on his say so and his belief in the veracity of his client responses, which he so carefully guides.

Notes:

[1] "Recovered Memories: Are They Reliable?" False Memory Syndrome Foundation, 3401 Market Street, Suite 130, Philadelphia, PA 19104-3318.

[2] Jay Haley. *Strategies of Psychotherapy*. New York: Grune & Stratton, Inc., 1963, p. 71.

[3] Michael D. Yapko. *Suggestions of Abuse: True and False Memories of Childhood Sexual Trauma*. New York: Simon & Schuster, 1994, p. 120.

[4] *Ibid.*, pp. 121, 122.

[5] William Watson. *A Concise Dictionary of Cults & Religions*. Chicago: Moody Press, 1991, p. 104. See also p. 247.

[6] Dave Hunt. *Occult Invasion*. Eugene, OR: harvest House Publishers, 1998, pp. 180-183.

[7] Alan Morrison. *The Serpent and the Cross: Religious Corruption in an Evil Age*. Birmingham, UK: K & M Books, 1994, p. 426.

[8] *Ibid.*, pp. 426, 427.

[9] *Ibid.*, p. 432.

[10] *Ibid.*, pp. 440, 441.

[11] *Ibid.*, p. 443.

[12] *Ibid.*, pp. 447, 448.

[13] E. Fuller Torrey. *The Mind Game*. New York: Emerson Hall Publishers, Inc., 1972, p. 69.

[14] *Self Hypnosis Tapes* Retail Catalogue. Grand Rapids: Potentials Unlimited, Inc., April, 1982.

[15] Yapko, *op. cit.*, p. 56.

[16] "Recovered Memories: Are They Reliable?" *op. cit.*

[17] Campbell Perry. *Hynos*, Vol. XXII, No. 4, p. 189.

[18] Mark Pendergrast. *Victims of Memory: Incest Accusations and Shattered Lives*. Hinesburg, VT: Upper Access, Inc., 1995, p. 129.

[19] *Ibid.*, p. 127.

[20] *Ibid.*, p. 128.

[21] *Ibid.*, p. 129.

[22] *Ibid.*

[23] Yapko, *op. cit.*, p. 54.

[24] *Ibid.*, p. 61.

6

Eye Movement Desensitization and Reprocessing and TheoPhostics

As mentioned earlier, there are similarities between a psychotherapy called *EMDR* (Eye Movement Desensitization and Reprocessing), developed by Dr. Francine Shapiro, and Smith's TheoPhostic therapy. The following is a brief description of EMDR from Shapiro's internet web site:

> The EMDR protocols guide clinicians to utilize specific history-taking procedures to ascertain (a) what earlier life experiences have contributed to the symptomatology, (b) what present triggers elicit the disturbance, and (c) what behaviors and skills are necessary to prepare the client for appropriate future action. For instance, the clinician identifies the specific events which taught the client such negative self-assessments as: I'm not good enough; I'm not lovable; I can't succeed; I'm worthless; I can't trust, etc. The assumption is that these earlier life experiences are stored in a dysfunctional fashion,

contributing to the client's inappropriate reactions in the present. Consistent with recent conjectures regarding memory (van der Kolk, 1994), it is believed that experiences which provide the underpinnings of pathology have been stored without sufficient processing. When these earlier experiences are brought to mind, they retain a significant level of disturbance, manifested by both emotions and physical sensations. Reprocessing these experiences with EMDR allows the client to gain insight, shift cognitive assessment, incorporate ecological emotions and body reactions, as well as adopt more adaptive behaviors.[1]

TheoPhostic counseling echoes much of the above description of EMDR, even though the process itself involves differences. Smith's TheoPhostic is also based on a theory of the mind similar to following description by Dr. Herbert Gravitz, an EMDR trained psychologist:

> EMDR is based on the theory that we are born with an information processing system, whose job is simply to digest and assimilate the events of our day. Trauma disrupts this innate information processing system and creates an imbalance among its parts.
>
> When we incur trauma, according to this theory, the brain goes into shock, and the trauma can become "frozen" in our nervous system. Information that may be inappropriate gets locked into the nervous system. We then experience in the present time the same kinds of feelings that were occurring at the time of the trauma.
>
> Because the original information stays stuck and can't move through the system, we continue to relive the experience. That may be why we seem unable to stop ourselves from repeating the same dysfunctional

behaviors over and over again despite "knowing" better.[2]

In their book *EMDR*, Shapiro and Margot Silk Forrest describe the process as follows:

> It appears that within each of us there is an infor-mation-processing system that is designed to process upsetting events so that we can maintain a state of mental health. When something unpleasant happens, we think about it, talk about it, and dream about it until it doesn't bother us anymore. At this stage, we can say it has arrived at an "adaptive resolution." We have learned whatever was useful about the experience (such as the danger of walking in dark alleys) and stored it in our brain with the appropri-ate emotion so it can guide us in the future. We have also discarded what is useless, such as the negative emotions, physical sensations, and self-beliefs that stemmed from the event.
>
> When something traumatic happens to us, however, this innate processing system can break down. Our perceptions of the terrible event (what we saw, heard, felt, and so on) may be stuck in our nervous system in the same form as when we expe-rienced them. These unprocessed perceptions can be expressed as the nightmares, flashbacks, and intru-sive thoughts of PTSD. In EMDR we ask the person to think of the traumatic event, and then we stimu-late the person's information-processing system so that the traumatic experience can be appropriately processed, or "digested." As this "digestion" process takes place, insights arise, the needed associations are made, whatever is useful is learned, and the appropriate emotions take over.[3]

In EMDR it is called the "traumatic event"; in TheoPhostics it is called the "historical memory event" (p. 37). The information-processing system in EMDR is not the same in TheoPhostics, but there is a parallel. Smith says:

> According to the Scriptures, negative emotions such as fear, depression, abandonment, shame, hopelessness, worry, anxiety and powerlessness are all the result of faulty thinking and misbelief (p. 40).

Except for the reference to Scripture, EMDR teachings are similar. Smith states, *"TheoPhostic* counseling can make it possible for a person to be relieved totally from all their shame and guilt" (p. 41). Replace the words *TheoPhostic counseling* with *EMDR* and the same claim is made by Shapiro. Both EMDR and TheoPhostic counseling offer relief from feelings of fear, shame, guilt, worry, anxiety and other negative emotions that they postulate as being the source of current pathology.

As with Smith's claims for TheoPhostic counseling, EMDR therapists assert that it is not unusual for EMDR to work in a brief amount of time in comparison with other therapies.[4]

Shapiro and Forrest say:

> Almost without exception, those treated with EMDR successfully resolved their traumatic memory in one session; the thought of it no longer disturbed them. In addition, they made huge leaps in the way they felt about themselves. My subjects shed their deep-rooted denial, fear, guilt, shame, and anger literally before my eyes and replaced these emotions with self-esteem, confidence, forgiveness, and acceptance. Measured by the frequent SUD ratings I took and the subjects' comments, the changes took place so

rapidly, I could *see* them. It was like watching free association at turbo speed.[5] (Italics hers.)

There are numerous similarities between EMDR and TheoPhostic counseling. Both have many cases of early life abuse and particularly of sexual abuse. In the TheoPhostic system the "three essential components of the process" are "the historical emotional 'echo,'" "the memory picture," and "the original lie" (pp. 35, 37, 46). EMDR functions with similar concepts and methods of revelation.

In describing "sexual assault victims," Shapiro and Forrest say:

In EMDR treatment, some of the negative self-beliefs therapists hear from sexual assault victims are "I am damaged for life," I am powerless," "I am bad," and "I am worthless." When a woman utters words such as these, she is not partaking in an intellectual exercise. She is verbalizing the emotion she feels when she thinks of the sexual assault or when memories of the attack are triggered. Although she may understand intellectually when friends or family remind her that she is now safe, this reassurance may make no dent on her automatic physiological response. As we observed with combat veterans, although the victim may have been in numerous group therapy sessions and read various self-help books, she is not able emotionally to incorporate the helpful information given to her. The high level of emotional disturbance is locked in her nervous system and chains her to the past event.

Although self-help techniques can show the rape victim how to cope better with her distress, they don't go far enough. The goal of EMDR therapy is for the victim to become entirely free of emotional turmoil.

The woman who is plagued with intrusive pictures of her rapist's face, the feeling of his hands on her body, and the heat of his breath on her face needs to process all of this information. When she has completed EMDR, these physical sensations and the negative emotions that go with them will no longer be stored in the memory network about the rape: They may be remembered as facts, but they will no longer be felt. With EMDR, part of the treatment includes facilitating the emotional adoption of positive self-beliefs such as "I'm now in control," "I am fine," "I did the best I could," "I am a worthwhile person," or "I now have choices." Once all of this has happened, the bonds of the past are essentially broken, and the rape survivor can take her proper place in the present.[6]

If one uses the above from EMDR as a template and then reads the abuse cases in Smith's manual on TheoPhostic counseling, the similarity will be amazing. The "negative self-beliefs" reported in EMDR, such as "I am damaged for life," "I am powerless," "I am bad," and "I am worthless," are similarly found in the TheoPhostic manual. Shapiro and Forrest say:

> When she has completed EMDR, these physical sensations and the negative emotions that go with them will no longer be stored in the memory network about the rape: They may be remembered as facts, but they will no longer be felt.[7]

One will see similar claims and nearly the same descriptions in the TheoPhostic counseling cases. The "positive self-beliefs" of EMDR, such as "I'm now in control," "I am fine," "I did the best I could," "I am a worthwhile person," or "I now have choices," are similarly found in the TheoPhostic counseling manual.

As an example of TheoPhostic counseling with a sexual assault victim, Smith tells of a woman named Paula, who approached him after a workshop (pp. 21-25). The process moves from an early memory picture to Paula reporting she was raped when a young girl. Paula reports, "I feel afraid, out of control and great terror." In addition she reports, "I feel dirty, nasty and shameful" (p. 22). After Smith uses his similar-to-EMDR "information processing system," Paula reports, "It's gone! The yucky stuff is gone! This is amazing!. . . I am not dirty. And it's over. I am safe now" (p. 24).

The many other abuse cases reported in the TheoPhostic manual are similar to this. Similar also are the many abuse cases in EMDR. Many other concepts and practices of EMDR are found in the TheoPhostic system. It is remarkable to see the likeness of the cases described in EMDR and those in the TheoPhostic manual. However, just as Smith uses psychoanalytic theories and techniques, absent the Oedipus complex, so too does Smith use the EMDR theories and techniques, absent the eye movements. Shapiro and Forrest report that there is research support that the unique combination of elements that make up EMDR provides an effective method of psychotherapy **even without the eye movements.**[8] (Bold added.)

If one removed all theories and techniques that originated from psychoanalysis, cognitive therapy, and EMDR out of TheoPhostic counseling, the system would collapse to a residue of inner healing practices similar to ones already being used, including demon deliverance. We are not saying that all the psychological concepts and activities we note are exactly duplicated in TheoPhostic counseling or that TheoPhostic counseling incorporates any of them in their entirety. However, it is transparent from the evidence that much of the true source of TheoPhostics is found in psychoanalysis, cognitive therapy and EMDR.

EMDR Rating Scales and TheoPhostic Counseling

At one time Shapiro used a scale called Subjective Units Disturbance (SUD) to measure her subjects' feelings. She describes SUD as:

> . . . a widely accepted tool developed forty years ago by Joseph Wolpe, a psychiatrist and renowned figure in behavioral therapy. To use the SUD, the subject thinks of a memory and rates how disturbing it feels on a scale from 0 to10, in which 0 is neutral, or no disturbance, and 10 is the greatest disturbance imaginable. For example, in my study, I might ask a combat veteran to remember a time he was ambushed by a Viet Cong soldier. Even though the incident happened twenty years ago, it could still be upsetting, and the subject might rate it at 8, 9, or 10. After EMDR treatment, the subject's SUD level should go down to 0 or 1, meaning that he could bring the ambush to mind and it no longer upset him.[9]

Shapiro later states:

> The scale I developed, and continue to use today, called for my subjects to rate how true their positive belief felt to them on a scale from 1 to 7, in which 1 means completely false and 7 means completely true. I also asked them to give me their gut-level response rather than tell me the way they thought they should feel. I called this measurement the Validity of Cognition (VOC) Scale. In general, people start EMDR treatment with a VOC of 4 or less. After doing EMDR, clients should report an increase in how true their

positive cognition (belief) feels; unless the VOC is at 6 or 7, the disturbing memory is not fully resolved.[10]

In the TheoPhostic manual Smith has a chapter titled "Rating the process." In the chapter he describes the "*TheoPhostic* Session Record Sheet (SRS) (p. 86). Just as EMDR focuses on memories of the past and associated emotions which emerge, so too does Smith's "Emotional Identification/Intensity Record" (EIIR), which is part of his SRS. Both the EMDR rating test and the TheoPhostic EIIR ask the client to rate the intensity of emotions. Smith says:

> The rating scale is "0-10." An "8' or above is a high rating and an indication of severe pain and traumatic damage. I prefer to get a rating of nine to ten and will often keep looking for that emotion which will cause the rating to move above an eight. When a person gives a rating of ten I know I am right on target (p. 88).

Smith also uses the scale for level of "believability." He says:

> The same ten point scale used to rate the emotional intensity is used to rate the believability of the lie where zero means "not true at all" and ten means "very true" (pp. 106, 107).

These rating scores are then recorded on the Session Record Sheet, which Smith describes as the:

> Record sheet that is used during the counseling session which keeps track of the ongoing therapy session. It is used to record the intensities of emotions and lies and the believability of lies. It also records

truths received and post-rate scales at the conclusion of the session (p. 283).

Smith describes his eventual therapeutic goal. He says:

> A rating of less than three means the person has received significant healing and a major shift has occurred. Though a three indicates good *progress do not accept anything more than a zero before you terminate the process* (p. 88).

As one reads the use of the scales in EMDR and in Smith's TheoPhostic system the similarities are readily transparent. Even a cursory comparison of the cases discussed, means of rating the intensity of emotions, and the very methodology used is too congruent between the two to be coincidental. In fact, if TheoPhostics had been in existence before EMDR, we would accuse Shapiro of obtaining her material from TheoPhostics. However, EMDR preceded TheoPhostics by a number of years. If there were only one psychotherapeutic system to choose from as evidence of the psychotherapeutic origin of TheoPhostic counseling, EMDR would be it.

Early Life Determinants, Freud, EMDR, and TheoPhostic Counseling

Freud believed that the unconscious portion of the mind, rather than the conscious, influences all of a person's thoughts and actions. In fact, he believed that the unconscious not only influences, but determines everything an individual does. Such psychic determinism was considered by Freud to be established within the unconscious during the first five years of life.

Morris Eagle, president of the American Psychological Association's psychoanalysis division, has said that one of Freud's core beliefs is that "our behavior, thoughts and emotions stem from unconscious fears and desires, often rooted in childhood experiences."[11]

Calvin Hall and Gardner Lindzey say:

> Freud was probably the first psychological theorist to emphasize the developmental aspects of personality and in particular to stress the decisive role of the early years of infancy and childhood in laying down the basic character structure of the person.[12]

Hall and Lindzey indicate that according to Freud:

> Personality develops in response to four major sources of tension: (1) physiological growth processes, (2) frustrations, (3) conflicts, and (4) threats. As a direct consequence of increases in tension emanating from these sources, the person is forced to learn new methods of reducing tension. This learning is what is meant by personality development.[13]

A number of major Freudian doctrines are found in EMDR. Shapiro and Forrest indicate at times their indebtedness to Freud. They say:

> The past affects the present even without our being aware of it. This knowledge is probably Freud's greatest gift to psychology, and thanks to the extremely rapid effects of EMDR, it is something I have witnessed again and again in working with people.[14]

Shapiro and Forrest repeat a number of times the relationship of early and present life. They say:

> Early life experiences, many of which took place in childhood, long before we had any choice, appear clinically to be one of the primary reasons for certain

kinds of depression, phobias, anxiety, stress, low self-esteem, relationship difficulties, and addictions.[15]

To understand clients more thoroughly, I often ask them to give me a list of the ten most disturbing events from their childhood.[16]

Unless the cause of the problem is organic, or bio-chemical, everything we feel or do, every action we take, is guided by previous life experiences, because all of them are linked together in an associative memory network.[17]

Although earlier life experiences are generally at the root of a pathological response in the present, they are given different clinical labels depending on the symptoms they cause.[18]

The thing to remember is that some of the fears we all face are merely earlier life experiences that are locked in our nervous system.[19]

There is no question that Smith shares the Freudian and EMDR penchant for the significance of early life experiences. As Smith therapizes individuals, he often speaks of "leading them to look back." Smith refers to "lies embedded in your memories" (p. 19). There are a number of places where Smith emphasizes how the early life dictates later choices in addition to "thinking and behaving." The following are just several of many such quotes:

When I "feel" in the present, I am actually remembering the past (p. 39).

More often than not their current pain is merely a reflection or an echo of their past (p. 39).

Their current issues are most always an echo or reflection of childhood wounds resurfacing in each individual's life brought on by the similarities of their current conflict (p. 232).

I believe every emotion we feel in the present is a preconceived interpretation, based upon an earlier memory event (p. 39).

The following statement by Smith reveals a controlling function in his therapy: "Most people are greatly surprised to discover how much of their daily lives are being dictated by what has happened in their earlier life" (p. 47). Smith says:

One of the primary roles I play as a therapist is to help people let go of the current difficulty and follow the emotion back to the original memory picture. Once the strong emotion in their present state is identified, I will ask them if they ever remember feeling this same emotion at an earlier time in their life (p. 44).

One very interesting early life exploration recommended by Smith is discussed under his section titled "Make one final sweep of their memories" (p. 191). Smith takes his clients through what he calls "Life Span Sweep," which he describes as "a process of accessing memories from early childhood all the way to the present in one broad sweep." He says:

I will have them close their eyes and imagine they are in their mother's womb awaiting birth. As they are visualizing being curled up in utero I ask them how they feel. Many will say safe and secure. Some will say they feel alone or unwanted (p. 191).

Smith does "not believe these are actual prebirth memories," but rather "feelings the child later felt about being
born which are being projected to this moment." Thus he
says, "We process these feelings and thoughts the same
way we do any other lie" (p. 191). Then, after having the
client experience prebirth feelings, Smith leads his clients
to spend time focusing on each year. He says, "Each
memory and lie is processed before we go to the next year."

Thus, while Smith does not believe in prebirth memories, he nevertheless processes these imagined prebirth
memories in the same way as other memories garnered
through this process. As a matter of fact, all memories in
the TheoPhostic system are processed as if true. The early
life determinants and the acceptance of early life memories as being factual and true are an integral part of
TheoPhostic counseling. Whether something is true or not
should be of paramount importance if God is involved in
the system, but in Smith's system false memories are
accepted and treated as true if they "feel" true, even when
the counselor knows they may not be true.

Smith has clearly immersed himself in the numerous psychotherapeutic theories and therapies as well as
in inner healing practices. Those theories, therapies, and
practices that place present problems of living in the past
and attempt to access the past through memories satu-
rate the entire TheoPhostic system to the degree that one
must conclude that Smith's counseling theories came from
human imagination rather than divine revelation. The
next two chapters demonstrate how loud the voice of Freud
comes through the TheoPhostic system.

Notes:

[1] Francine Shapiro. "EMDR in Brief," <http://www.emdr.com>. Palo
Alto, CA: Mental Research Institute, 1994.

[2] Herbert Gravitz quoted by Marilyn McMahon in "The eyes have it:
controversial therapy gaining respect." *Santa Barbara News-Press*,
June 25, 1996, pp. B6, B8.

3 Francine Shapiro and Margot Silk Forrest. *EMDR: The Break-through "Eye Movement" Therapy for Overcoming Anxiety, Stress, and Trauma.* New York: Basic Books, 1997, pp. 28, 29.

4 McMahon, *ibid.*, p. B8.

5 *Ibid.*, p. 18.

6 *Ibid.*, pp. 134, 135.

7 *Ibid.*, p. 135.

8 *Ibid.*, p. vii.

9 *Ibid.* p. 17.

10 *Ibid.*

11 Morris Eagle quoted by John Horgan, "Why Freud Isn't Dead," *Scientific American*, December 1996, pp. 74-79.

12 Calvin S. Hall and Gardner Lindzey. *Theories of Personality.* New York: John Wiley & Sons, Inc., 1957, p. 46.

13 *Ibid.*, p. 46.

14 Francine Shapiro and Margot Silk Forrest. *EMDR: The Break-through "Eye Movement" Therapy for Overcoming Anxiety, Stress, and Trauma.* New York: Basic Books, 1997, p. 47.

15 *Ibid.*, p. 29.

16 *Ibid.*, p. 51.

17 *Ibid.*, p. 66.

18 *Ibid.*, p. 66.

19 *Ibid.*, p. 242.

7

Freud's Psychoanalysis and TheoPhostics

Freudian psychoanalytic (psychodynamic) therapy is the source for many later therapies and a major influence in TheoPhostic counseling. We will give a general description of psychoanalytic (Freudian) therapy, describe elements of it, and then demonstrate its use in TheoPhostic counseling.

Psychoanalysis (Freud)

Sigmund Freud is the most prominent name in psychotherapy. He is not only considered the father of the psychotherapy movement, but his ideas also permeate later theories and therapies.

> Probably no single individual has had a more profound effect on twentieth-century thought than Sigmund Freud. His works have influenced psychiatry, anthropology, social work, penology, and education and provided a seemingly limitless source of material for novelists and dramatists. Freud has

111

created a "whole new climate of opinion"; for better or worse he has changed the face of society.[1]

Although many of Freud's ideas are under attack by a number of critics, he still remains one of the most influential of all psychological theorists. An article in *Scientific American* tells "Why Freud Isn't Dead."[2] The article demonstrates Freud's continuing influence even though some specific Freudian ideas, such as the Oedipus complex, have "fallen out of favor even among psychoanalysts." Morris Eagle, president of the American Psychological Association's psychoanalysis division and professor at Adelphi University says, "There are very few analysts who follow all of Freud's formulations."[3] The *Scientific American* article goes on to state:

> Nevertheless, psychotherapists of all stripes still tend to share two of Freud's core beliefs: One is that our behavior, thoughts and emotions stem from unconscious fears and desires, often rooted in childhood experiences. The other is that with the help of a trained therapist, we can understand the source of our troubles and thereby obtain some relief.[4]

Besides sharing the two "core beliefs" of Freud, Smith uses many Freudian theories, techniques and methods. Like many therapists, Smith has jettisoned Freud's Oedipal theory. However, Smith is nonetheless dependent on Freudian psychology. We want to make it clear that the concepts are not all exactly the same. However, we are saying that psychology is the true source of much of TheoPhostic counseling.

TheoPhostic and the Freudian Unconscious
In Freud's psychoanalytic theory he describes the mind as having two compartments. One portion of the mind is

the conscious and the other the unconscious. Freud developed a complex set of theories to describe personality and to attempt to understand and treat mental-emotional disorders. Basic to these theories is his description of the unconscious portion of the mind as that part of the psyche which is hidden from the person himself and not open to direct knowledge. The usual analogy is that of an iceberg, with most of the mind submerged, hidden, and filled with a vast amount of powerful, motivating material.

Smith says, "As God was revealing this method to me one of the ways He made it known was through an analogy I have come to identify as the 'two room house.'" He continues:

> One room is bright and clear with the lights turned on. This room contains the logical truth about the event and the logical truths about the innocence of the children who are molested. . . . Next to this first room there is another room with the lights turned off. This room contains the original memories and embedded lies which shamed them, causing deep feelings of guilt, hopelessness and despair (p. 32).

TheoPhostic's "light room" is like Freud's tip of the iceberg; Smith's "dark room" is like the part below the waterline. With psychoanalysis, the unconscious is the "room" containing the memories that are hidden and must be accessed for relief to occur. With TheoPhostic it is the "dark room" that contains the memories that are hidden and must be accessed for relief to occur.

Smith says:

> The dark room is the location in the brain where the actual traumatic memory data has been encoded and stored. . . . In the dark room the memory also contains the early interpretations of the event (pp. 32, 33).

The dark room of TheoPhostic is the center stage upon which the most important dramatic elements are focused, just as with the unconscious in Freudian psychology.

Freudian Defense Mechanisms and TheoPhostics

According to Dr. Ernest Hilgard et al., "Freud used the term defense mechanisms to refer to unconscious processes that defend a person against anxiety by distorting reality in some way . . . they all involve an element of self-deception."[5] The *Concise Encyclopedia of Psychology* defines them this way:

> *Defense mechanisms* are psychological strategies by which persons reduce or avoid negative states such as conflict, frustration, anxiety, and stress. Because it is assumed that most people are motivated to reduce these negative states, theorists have devoted considerable attention to the identification of defense mechanisms, and a wide variety of mechanisms have been suggested. Most of the theorizing concerning the defense mechanisms has been provided by psychodynamically oriented individuals, primarily S. Freud. . . . Three points should be recognized concerning the defenses in general. First, defense mechanisms are used *to avoid or reduce negative emotional states*. Second, most defense mechanisms involve a *distortion of reality*. Third, persons are *usually not consciously aware of their use of most defense mechanisms*.[6] (Italics theirs.)

Calvin Hall and Gardner Lindzey say: "All defense mechanisms have two characteristics in common: (1) they deny, falsify, or distort reality, and (2) they operate unconsciously so that the person is not aware of what is taking place."[7]

Smith knows the Freudian defense mechanisms and refers to them many times in the TheoPhostic manual. In discussing one of the components of his system, Smith says: "Logic is the cause of the defense mechanisms which have kept them from accessing their wounds and healing" (p. 56).

Under "Cloned lies," Smith explains the *"active memory principle."* He says, "'Active' memories are accessed apart from the person's choice. This is an automatic reflex of the brain as it protects the individual from pain" (p. 63). According to Smith's system, these memories are stored in the "dark room" (unconscious) and rise up or influence the person's thoughts and life "apart from the person's choice." This "automatic reflex of the brain" which "protects the individual from pain" is a loud echo if not a clone of the Freudian unconscious and defense mechanisms. Smith's system uses Freudian ideas of the unconscious and Freudian defense mechanisms. Smith says:

> Some of you may see these types of lies as what some call defense mechanisms. You are correct in your assumption. These defenses are mental processes that guard us from accessing the root problems. These are all sinful (less than God's intention) attempts at healing ourselves through things such as denial, suppression, projection, sublimation, minimizing and justification (p. 67).

While a number of the Freudian ego-defense mechanisms are evident in TheoPhostic counseling, the following, as described in the *Concise Encyclopedia of Psychology*, play an important role in Smith's work:

> **Repression** is the selective forgetting of material associated with conflict and stress. Repression serves as a defense because, if a person is not aware of the

conflictive and stressful material, the conflict and stress will not exist for the person. There are three important things to note about repression. First, repression is *motivated selective forgetting*. It is a loss designed to selectively eliminate from consciousness the memories or related associations that cause the individual to experience conflict or stress. Second, repressed material is not lost but rather *stored in the unconscious*. If for some reason the negative feeling associated with the material is eliminated, the once repressed material can return to consciousness without having to be relearned. Third, Freud postulated two types of repression. The first type was *primal repression*, which involves a "denial of entry into consciousness" of threatening material. In this type of repression it appears as if the individual did not even perceive the material. Freud called the second type of repression *proper* or *afterexpulsion*. Once recognized, however, the material is repressed and the person is no longer aware of the material.

Repression is undoubtedly one of the most important concepts in the areas of personality and psychopathology. Indeed, the existence of repression is a prerequisite for the development of an unconscious because . . . it is through repression that material supposedly enters the unconscious. . . .

In **suppression**, the person avoids stressful thoughts by not thinking about them. Because it is difficult not to think, suppression usually involves thinking about other non-stressful things that can replace the stressful thoughts, causing some researchers to refer to this as *avoidant thinking* or *attentional diversion*. Suppression differs from repression in that with suppression the stress-provoking thought is available but is ignored and blocked by other thoughts, rather than being completely unavailable as is the case with repression. . . .

In **denial**, a person does not attend to the threat-provoking aspects of a situation and changes the interpretation of the situation so as to perceive it as less threatening.
Denial differs from repression in that the person selectively attends and reinterprets, rather than obliterates, the experience from consciousness. Insofar as denial involves some selective attention, the process involves some amount of suppression. . . .[8] (Italics in original; bold added.)

The above descriptions of *repression*, *suppression*, and *denial* are all according to Freud and other psychodynamic theorists. They are ideas, not proven realities.

Smith defines "Suppression/repression" in his "Glossary of Terms" as follows:

Suppression is the active attempt to block out or bury painful thoughts and feelings. Repression is the unconscious success of having buried a thought or feeling and no ability to retrieve it willfully. Repressed memory is no longer accessible at will. These memories often hold the original lie (p. 281).

In his section on "The memory picture," Smith says, "These surfacing emotions are merely 'echoes' of long suppressed (possibly repressed) memories." In the next paragraph Smith says, "Often the memory which is producing the pain is buried deeply in the inner recesses of the mind" (p. 37). In his "Visual memory" section, Smith says, "There are some memories which are visually repressed and you will have to access the memory at an emotional or physical level void of visual imagery" (p. 38).

Several more of Smith's many references to the defense mechanisms are:

> She had repressed the sexual abuse but could not suppress the emotional feeling coming from the repressed lie (p. 53).

> These coping skills [defense mechanisms], unconsciously developed by the person, are major barriers standing in the way of the process (p. 116).

> As time passes, people tend to suppress the memories by blocking them out each time they surface. At some point, some are even successful in repressing them beyond access. Successful repression does not mean escape from the destruction and devastation which the embedded lies created in such memories (p. 123).

> These very defenses which were created to protect them from further pain is walling them off and excluding them from God's healing touch. They are in essence a vain attempt to heal oneself through denial, suppression and avoidance (p. 130).

> The act of suppression and repression is nothing more than burying our wounds . . . (p. 131).

> A person can repress their wound so deeply that they will not be able to remember where they even buried it (p. 152).

> Repressed memories are as powerful and dictating as conscious memories. A person may succeed in suppressing their memories into repression and even

forget they ever happened, yet the lie and the memory can access the person anytime they want (p. 153).

It never goes away or loses its intensity; it merely goes deeper into repression (p. 157).

They have developed refined processes of denial and suppression that have built a thick wall between their conscious thinking and the traumatic event. As long as the thought has been suppressed the person does not have to deal with it. These coping or defense mechanisms are, at their root, acts of self preservation and self cure (p. 250).

The Freudian ego-defense mechanisms are obviously known to Smith and are an important part of the TheoPhostic process.

Freudian Id, Ego, Superego and TheoPhostics

According to Freud, the personality is made up of three major systems called the *id*, *ego*, and *superego*. Smith would be familiar with these three systems and their functions. TheoPhostic counseling reflects Smith's use of ideas from these three Freudian systems. We want to make it clear that the comparison is being made on the function of these systems and not on their location.

Id and Ego

According to Hall and Lindzey's book *Theories of Personality*, "Freud called the id the 'true psychic reality' because it represents the inner world of subjective experience and has no knowledge of objective reality. . . . The ego comes into existence because the needs of the organism require appropriate transactions with the objective world of reality."[9] While there are differences between the Freudian and TheoPhostic personality systems, there are similarities that reflect Smith's Freudian knowledge and use. Think of the id and what occurs in Smith's "dark room" and the ego and what occurs in Smith's "light room."

Smith describes three basic components of TheoPhostic as the "historical emotional 'echo,'" the "memory picture," and the "original lie" (pp. 35, 37, 46).

The Historical Emotional Echo. Smith says, "This emotional echo is the feeling the person experiences each time their painful memory is accessed . . . their present discomfort is rooted in an unresolved historical moment" (pp. 35, 36). The person is aware (conscious, light room, ego) of an earlier experienced "historical moment" (unconscious, dark room, id).

The Memory Picture. Smith refers to "the historical memory picture which matches the emotional echo" (p. 37). Smith directs counselors to "find the historical memory event which feels the same way or matches the emotions they are currently feeling" (p. 37). Current feeling (conscious, light room, ego); historical memory (unconscious, dark room, id).

The Original Lie. Smith says, "the lie is the belief statement which was planted in the person's mind during the time of the trauma" (p. 46). The original lie exists in the dark room (unconscious, id). There is not an exact likeness of the light room to the Freudian ego and consciousness nor an exact congruity between the dark room and the Freudian id and unconscious, but these psychoanalytic concepts are evident in TheoPhostic counseling.

Superego

Hall and Lindzey describe the superego as follows:

> It is the internal representative of the traditional values and ideals of society as interpreted to the child by his parents, and enforced by means of a system of rewards and punishments imposed upon the child.

The superego is the moral arm of personality; it represents the ideal rather than the real and it strives for perfection rather than pleasure. Its main concern is to decide whether something is right or wrong so that it can act in accordance with the moral standards authorized by the agents of society.

The superego as the internalized moral arbiter of conduct develops in the response to the rewards and punishments meted out by the parents. To obtain the rewards and avoid the punishments, the child learns to guide his behavior along the lines laid down by the parents. Whatever they say is improper and punish him for doing tends to become incorporated into his *conscience*.[10]

Smith says:

An important aspect of the mind/soul is seen in the function of what some call the conscience. The primary purpose of the soul/conscience is to keep us on the straight and narrow. Its task is to reward us or punish us as we choose to obey or violate the information it contains. As long as I obey the core truths in my conscience I will feel a sense of well being. But if I violate my conscience I will feel guilt or conviction (p. 174).

Later in the same section, Smith says:

The conscience received its original false information through two basic means. When a person is exposed to the same information over and over for a long extended period of time such information is eventually embraced as truth whether it be factual or not. . . .

Another means by which lies are embedded into our
conscience is through traumatic events. If I am being
sexually assaulted as a child, the thoughts or interpretation made during the event will be implanted
in my conscience (p. 178).

Smith's description of the origin and operation of the
conscience in TheoPhostic counseling reflects that of the
Freudian superego enough to be one more clue as to the
roots of his system. Although he renames them, Smith's
use of the Freudian id, ego, and superego are transparent
and evident.

When referring to the id, ego, and superego, Hall and
Lindzey say, "Behavior is nearly always the product of an
interaction among these three systems; rarely does one
system operate to the exclusion of the other two."[11] This is
also true of Smith's equivalence of the id, ego, and superego in TheoPhostic. One source for the TheoPhostic structure of personality is no doubt Freud. Over a period of
time Freud's views on the id, ego, and superego did vary,
but when one compares the Freudian structure of personality in its original or modified forms with TheoPhostic,
there is an obvious relationship.

Notes:

[1] E. M. Thornton. *The Freudian Fallacy.* Garden City: The Dial Press,
Doubleday and Company, 1984, p. ix.

[2] John Horgan. "Why Freud Isn't Dead," *Scientific American,* December 1996, pp. 74-79.

[3] *Ibid.,* p. 74.

[4] *Ibid.*

[5] Ernest Hilgard, Richard Atkinson, Rita Atkinson. *Introduction to
Psychology,* Seventh Edition. New York: Harcourt, Brace, Jovanovich,
Inc., 1979, p. 427.

6 Raymond J. Corsini and Alan J. Auerbach. *Concise Encyclopedia of Psychology.* New York: John Wiley & Sons, Inc., 1996, 1998, pp. 208-209.

7 Calvin S. Hall and Gardner Lindzey. *Theories of Personality.* New York: John Wiley & Sons, Inc., 1957, p. 49.

8 Corsini and Auerbach, *op. cit.*, p. 209.

9 Hall and Lindzey, *op. cit.,* pp. 33, 34.

10 *Ibid.*, p. 35.

11 *Ibid.*, p. 32.

8

Freud's Dynamics and TheoPhostics

Freudian Free Association and TheoPhostics

Freud developed the technique of free association, which is the central activity of psychoanalysis. In free association the patient reveals his thought life through unrestrained verbalizations. Through this process the individual is theoretically unveiling his unconscious to the analyst, who in turn supposedly gains deep understanding of the patient's psyche.

In discussing free association, *The Oxford Companion to the Mind* says, "In 1912, in the *Dynamics of Transference*, [Freud] described his fundamental principle of psychoanalysis as the requirement that the patient repeats whatever comes into his or her head without criticizing it."[1]

A Dictionary for Psychotherapists states:

> Free association is extremely difficult because we are all socially trained not to reveal a substantial portion of our thoughts. Some analysts have quipped

that when a patient can free associate properly, the analysis is over; a great deal of analytic work consists of dealing with resistances to free association. The term "free," of course, refers to the patient being asked to suspend conscious control and to express verbally each thought and feeling, as well as sensation, image and memory, without reservation as it spontaneously occurs. This is sometimes referred to as the fundamental rule of psychoanalysis and requires the patient to overcome the usual conscious embarrassment, fear, shame, and guilt. The interventions of the analyst's interpreting defenses hopefully removes these defenses and allows more material to bubble up into the patient's conscious and be expressed through free association.[2]

Smith's "drifting" technique is an imprint of Freudian free association. Smith says:

When in pursuit of the original lie and memory, the person is led to focus on the current life situation that is producing the strong emotion. After they have focused on their current situation they are asked to focus on the emotion it is producing, and allow the emotion to become the primary focal point. As they do this they are asked to disconnect from the current memory picture and "drift" backward through time (p. 276).

Smith not only asks individuals to "drift back"; he also uses other expressions that relate to free association, such as "feel around" and "look back," where further directions are not given and restraints are not suggested (pp. 66, 161).

Smith describes *"secondary memories,"* which "contain feelings which are common with the original memory and wound," and says, "The reason these secondary memories feel like the original wound is due to the 'cloning' of the original lie" (p.44). He says, "Whenever I sense a memory a client locates is not the original memory, I only pay it a temporary visit" (p. 45). To locate the original lie, the client is directed to look for what Smith believes is an original memory. To reach this original memory or lie, Smith says:

> I ask him to "drift" back through time and allow his memories to surface. I ask him not to look for a memory but simply drift and focus on the emotion of the memory. . . . I try to place no restraints on their drifting (p. 45).

Then he instructs his readers, "When you come to an early childhood memory or are unable to move any further back by 'drifting,' explore the memory and begin the healing process" (p. 45). The object of this drifting, as with free association, is to find an original memory. In TheoPhostic counseling the purpose is to confront the original lie hidden in the "dark room," which would be the unconscious in Freudian psychology.

Smith says:

> Discerning the original lie in the client's memory picture is the most difficult part of this process. There are endless possibilities of what the lie might be in any given memory picture but only discovering the original lies will work. You will have to act like a detective at a crime scene looking for clues (p. 101).

Drifting, like free association, produces many images, memories, and thoughts. However, Smith's intent is to lead the client "right back into their original memory with all its pain" (p. 107). As we discussed earlier, the client's original memory is most often an early life memory. This

is also what Freudian analysts look for. As one compares
drifting with free association, it is not an exact clone, but
enough of a reflection to identify its psychological source.
Although Smith recommends and prescribes drifting
(a form of free association) to his clients, he additionally
is very directive about the therapy he performs. In other
words, Smith encourages drifting (free association), but
he also makes suggestions along the way and guides the
formation of the imagery. We have already refuted Smith's
claim to having a nondirective role, which is contradicted
by his very own words.

Freudian Abreaction/Catharsis & Stirring Up the Darkness

The *Dictionary of Psychology* describes abreaction and
catharsis as follows:

> **abreaction:** (*Psychoan.*) the discharge of tension by
> reliving in words, feeling and actions a traumatic
> experience (the original cause of the tension) in the
> presence of an analyst. *Syn.* CATHARSIS. (*Abreaction*
> is the preferred technical term; *catharsis* is used more
> in non-technical writing.)[3]

> **catharsis:** (*Psychoan.*) the release of tensions and
> anxieties by reliving and unburdening those trau-
> matic incidents which, in the past, were originally
> associated with the repression of the emotions. *Syn.*
> ABREACTION.[4]

The *Concise Encyclopedia of Psychology* states the following:

> According to C. Thompson, Freud "established abre-
> action through free association as a means of undo-
> ing the process of repression."[5]

Freud stated that the cathartic method [abreaction] was both the precursor and the ongoing nucleus of psychoanalysis.[6]

A Dictionary for Psychotherapists says that *abreaction* "represents the discharge of emotion that was attached to a previously repressed memory as it emerges into the consciousness."[7]

The Oxford Companion to the Mind describes *abreaction* as:

> A recalling or re-experiencing of stressful or disturbing situations or events which appear to have precipitated a neurosis. During the recalling the patient is encouraged to give an uninhibited display of emotion and afterwards it is hoped that the neurosis will have vanished.[8]

The cathartic method of abreaction was originally developed by Joseph Breuer, who employed this method in concert with hypnosis. Adolf Grünbaum refers to "Freud's own innovative psychoanalytic version of Breuer's method, which replaced hypnosis by the technique of free association to treat psychoneurotics."[9] Grünbaum also says:

> Incidentally, despite the innovative replacement of hypnosis by free association to recover repressed mentation in psychoanalytic treatment, Freudian therapy has retained an important tenet of its cathartic predecessor: "Recollection without affect almost invariably produces no [therapeutic] result."[10]

Smith defines "stirring up the darkness" by saying:

When the client focuses on the memory picture, taunts themselves with the original lie, and allows the strong emotions to surface, a "darkness" or hopelessness, powerlessness, shamefulness surrounds them. This is very traumatic during the few moments it occurs but is quickly elevated when the person receives the "light" of truth (p. 281).

Smith declares:

Probably the most radical shift in my counseling approach is in what I have come to call "*stirring up the darkness.*" . . . When I lead a client in this they are put right back into their original memory with all of its pain. . . . Now I encourage them to immerse themselves deeply into the painful memory and tell themselves the lies which are causing so much pain. I have come to realize the more they can "stir the darkness" the more intense the light of the truth becomes when God speaks (p. 107).

Smith gives examples of how he helps. He says:

I will often join in the "stirring" by saying things like "feel how dirty you are for..." "feel the panic and terror of knowing you cannot get away..." "feel how guilty you are for letting him..." (p. 108, ellipses in original).

Sprinkled throughout the TheoPhostic manual is the use of "stirring up the darkness." Associated with the stirring up are intense feelings, such as anger, hate, revenge, fear and other negative emotions. Much sharp, intense pain is also involved. The darkness from the stirring is often contrasted with light. Two contrasts follow: "The more you can stir up the darkness the more intense the light" (p. 237); "I have found the more intense the moment the more intense the truth that is experienced" (pp. 249, 250). A good example of the goal of the stirring is: "Stirring up the darkness opens up the wound and allows the deeply painful memories to surface" (p. 250).

Three Basic Components of Smith's TheoPhostic System and Abreaction

Smith claims, "If you match three you really do win; true healing and restoration" (p. 35). The first of the three basic components of TheoPhostic counseling is the "historical emotional 'echo'" (p. 35). Smith says:

> This emotional echo is the feeling the person experiences each time their painful memory is accessed . . . it is an emotional reflection of a previously felt event. . . . but I am convinced their present discomfort is rooted in an unresolved historical moment (pp. 35, 36).

Smith reveals the resistance that may occur in TheoPhostic counseling. He says:

> Helping people to disconnect from their current situation and leading them to look back to the original wound, is one of the greatest roadblocks the counselor will face in this process (p. 35).

Smith concludes this section by saying, "Their present situation is not the source of their pain but rather the trigger which has opened the window of their former wounds" (p. 37).

The second basic component is the "memory picture." Smith says "the historical memory picture" matches "the emotional echo" (p. 37). The counselor is to help the client "find the historical memory event which feels the same

way or matches the emotions they are currently feeling"
(p. 37). He contends, "These surfacing emotions are merely
'echoes' of long suppressed (possibly repressed) memories"
(p. 37). Smith stresses how important he thinks it is to
deal with the "unresolved historical pain" and says, "Often the memory which is producing the pain is buried
deeply in the inner recesses of the mind" (p. 37).

The third component in the TheoPhostic process is the
"original lie." Smith says:

> The lie is the belief statement which was planted in
> the person's mind during the time of the trauma. . . .
> The lie is the most difficult component of the three
> way match to identify, and to a great extent the most
> crucial (p. 46).

In his section "Discerning the original lie," Smith says:

> Since we are in the process of healing, the wounds
> remaining are still active and hinder our walk. . . .
> The controlling factor which hinders our life is not
> in the memory itself, but the lies (false interpreta-
> tions given about the event) embedded in the wound.
> To a great extent these lies affect us beyond our
> awareness (p. 48).

Throughtout Smith's explanation of the three essential concepts of TheoPhostic counseling, one repeatedly
reads of emotions, wounds, feelings, and pain in each con-
cept and in each explanation. Smith explains that he wants
the client to "revisit their memories and reexperience their
original pain." He explains why:

> I have discovered the more pain you can cause to
> surface from the original wound and the more in-
> tense and believable you can make the lie, the more

dramatic the truth becomes when it is spoken from God. The darker the room the more intense the light. . . . I seek to stir up the darkness and encourage the person to immerse themselves as deeply as they can in this darkness. It is in this painful and excruciating state that God is most clearly understood. If the person is not put in the [dark] room where the memory and lie reside, healing may never occur, or at best occur at a very slow rate (p. 55).

According to Smith TheoPhostic "is a healing moment."[11] Smith claims, "Emotionally hurting people from all walks of life, with all manner of emotional woundedness, consistently experience *accelerated healing* as truth replaces lies, freeing them from lifelong emotional/psychological pain."[12] Stirring up the darkness with its "healing moment" and accompanying intensity of feelings, emotions, and pain are too similar to the cathartic "moment" of psychoanalysis. Read cases from both therapeutic systems and the likeness will be abundantly evident.

"Stirring up the darkness" will be an intense emotional experience during TheoPhostic counseling. The person will feel something is really happening and emotionally expect healing to come when he reaches that climax of intensity. He has been prompted to hear directly from God at this point. **However, one must ask whether the verbal repetition of what Smith calls the "original lie" and the accompanying intense emotion are conducive to hearing God or whether they may actually facilitate hearing from demons?**

Notes:
[1] Richard L. Gregory, ed. *The Oxford Companion to the Mind.* Oxford: Oxford University Press, 1987, p. 266.

² Richard Chessick. *A Dictionary for Psychotherapists: Dynamic Concepts in Psychotherapy.* Northvale, NJ: Jason Aronson, Inc., 1993, p. 125.

³ J. P. Chaplin. *Dictionary of Psychology*, New Revised Edition. New York: Dell Publishing Company, Inc., 1975, p. 2.

⁴ *Ibid.*, p. 78.

⁵ Raymond J. Corsini and Alan J. Auerbach, eds. *Concise Encyclopedia of Psychology*, Second Edition, Abridged. New York: John Wiley & Sons, Inc., 1998, p. 1.

⁶ *Ibid.*, p. 106.

⁷ Chessick, *op. cit.*, p. 2.

⁸ Gregory, *op. cit.*, p. 1.

⁹ Adolph Grünbaum. *The Foundations of Psychoanalysis.* Berkeley: University of California Press, 1984, p. 148.

¹⁰ *Ibid.*, p. 185.

¹¹ Ed M. Smith. "Breakthroughs in Biblical Counseling and Genuine Inner Healing." FAX regarding TheoPhostic Training Seminars, Campbellsville, KY, p. 2.

¹² *Ibid.*, p. 4.

9

God's Sufficient Provision

Throughout the twentieth century psychological ideas of Freud and others have greatly influenced the way the world thinks. Moreover their ideas have seeped into the church both directly and indirectly through sermons, books, radio, seminars, Bible colleges and seminaries. We have seen the intrusion accelerate over the past three decades to the degree that psychological thinking often takes precedence over biblical thinking, meeting one's emotional needs seems more pressing than seeking the kingdom of God, increasing one's self-esteem is more avidly sought than humbling oneself under the mighty hand of God, and counseling is more often recommended than taking up one's cross. Along with the psychological intrusion has come an emphasis on feelings and an acceptance of extrabiblical religious experiences and practices. For many, the meaning of divine revelation has changed from a closed Canon of Scripture to whatever comes to mind under certain circumstances and engendered expectations.

With these changes in place, TheoPhostic counseling will appeal to many Christians who are looking for a way to help themselves and others who are hurting. Besides Smith's claim that *"TheoPhostic* counseling is a process of divinely accomplished miracles," the theory is simple and the system is easy to learn. One merely has to understand that the presenting problem is due to a "lie" embedded in an early life memory and that people act according to powerful material in the unconscious, which Smith calls the "dark room," in contrast to the conscious mind which he calls the "light room." He defines the "lie" as the interpretation one has given to a past event and says that "every emotion we feel in the present is a preconceived interpretation, based upon an earlier memory event" (p. 39). The counselor's main job is to convince the client of the usefulness of this system, to get past interferences such as logical and rational thinking, to gain the client's trust, and then to instruct the client to feel the emotion associated with the presenting problem and to "drift" back to earlier events that felt the same way.

When the person has reached an early memory (the earlier the better according to Smith) and described the feelings and memory, the counselor must "discern the lie" (p. 31). When the counselor discerns the "lie," it is his job to "stir up the darkness" by goading the client to repeat the "lie" over and over again until the emotions reach an intense climax. At this pitch of emotion intensified by repeating the "lie," clients are directed to listen for God to speak truth directly to them. However, there is no example in Scripture of the God of truth requiring a person to embrace and speak a "lie" to hear truth. It sounds more diabolical than divine. After this process, which is similar to Freudian abreaction, the client, believing that God has spoken, supposedly receives "complete recovery," but only from that particular "lie" (p. 7). One cannot know how many times this same gruesome, abreaction-like process will be repeated before all the "lies" supposedly embedded in different memories are exhumed.

Smith has put God in a TheoPhostic box, because he says that "God will not speak His truth" if the counselor has "not correctly identified the original lie" (p. 76). Thus God's hands are tied and His mouth is shut without the expert, the TheoPhostic counselor who has mastered Smith's system. Smith says the counselor "must discover 'the lie' that matches 'the picture' and stir up the accompanying emotion" so that the client can hear "the divine truth" (p. 57).

Smith's system is dependent on several different sources: (1) psychotherapeutic theories devised by nonChristians, (2) inner healing techniques which themselves are based on false psychotherapeutic theories of memory as well as on the occult, and (3) extra-biblical demon deliverance teachings and techniques. Smith not only uses secular psychotherapeutic sources for his system; he also suggests the possibility of using other forms of psychotherapy after the person has been healed of the "lies" (p. 11). In other words TheoPhostic counseling may not be enough for every client, but may need to be supplemented with additional psychotherapy. TheoPhostic is completely tied to psychotherapeutic theories and techniques in both its form and its practice. Furthermore, there is no external, third-party research evidence to prove that the system does what Smith claims or that any of this is more than a cathartic charade.

When one considers the wonder of what God has accomplished for believers and the vast provisions He has made for salvation, which includes justification, sanctification, and future glorification, one wonders why anyone must add to God's sufficient and abundant provision. Yes, we understand that Smith believes that TheoPhostic is part of God's provision, but it is not found in the Word of God and it is based on ungodly psychological systems comprised of the wisdom of men about which we are warned in 1 Corinthians 2. The Bible does not support Smith's system. In his vain attempt to biblicize his recently devised system, Smith eisegetes Scripture, resorts to metaphorical interpretation, and makes applications that have nothing to do with the intended meaning of the verses he cites.

God did not leave His children without sufficient supply throughout the centuries of the church age. His provisions for life and godliness are resident in Himself and graciously given to believers through His written revelation, the Bible, and through His indwelling Holy Spirit, who applies that Word to believers' lives. True Christians live by grace through faith in the resurrected Christ, knowing that their lives are eternally connected to Him and that He is presently working His good pleasure in them to conform them to the image of Christ, even through difficult circumstances (Romans 8:28-29).

When problems arise Christians have great opportunities to draw closer to God by believing His Word and growing in their faith in what He has already done and is doing in their lives, knowing that God will complete that which He has begun in Christ Jesus. Trusting God in the midst of trial is an essential part of sanctification and is the way of the Christian. In contrast, trusting in psychological, philosophical, or even spiritual systems devised by men is equivalent to the Israelites turning to idols for help rather than fully trusting God. However, few in the church realize the danger of turning to psychological counseling or other man-made systems to help them in their distress. They do not see how doing that is as serious as worshipping idols.

When the Israelites attempted to blend faith in God with trust in idols, they continued to be religious and to follow certain ceremonial rites. But their hope for help was divided. Instead of looking to God in faith and obedience, they adopted techniques that seemed to work for the pagan nations around them. The more they resorted to these outside methods of help, the more God was displeased with them. Jeremiah 2:11-13 records God's concern for those who turn to other sources of help:

> Hath a nation changed their gods, which are yet no gods? but my people have changed their glory for that which doth not profit. Be astonished, O ye heavens, at this, and be horribly afraid, be ye very desolate, saith the LORD. For my people have committed two evils; they have forsaken me the fountain of living waters, and hewed out cisterns, broken cisterns, that can hold no water.

The Israelites used the notions and methods of the heathen nations. Like those who attempt to use both psychotherapy and the Bible, they sought to increase their help by practicing idolatry as well as worshipping God. But, God declared those who trust in man as being cursed:

> Thus saith the LORD, Cursed be the man that trusteth in man, and maketh flesh his arm, and whose heart departeth from the LORD... (Jeremiah 17:5).

Yet, if they turn to God and trust Him, they are blessed:

> Blessed is the man that trusteth in the LORD, and whose hope the LORD is. For he shall be as a tree planted by the waters, and that spreadeth out her roots by the river, and shall not see when heat cometh, but her leaf shall be green; and shall not be careful in the year of drought, neither shall cease from yielding fruit. The heart is deceitful above all things, and desperately wicked: who can know it? I the LORD search the heart, I try the reins, even to give every man according to his ways, and according to the fruit of his doings (Jeremiah 17:7-10).

No psychologically based system, TheoPhostic counseling or any other unholy mixture, can know the heart of man, no matter how many theories and therapies are devised. Only God knows the heart, and God is a rewarder of those who trust in Him (Hebrews 4:12-13 and 11:6). No system can change the inner man the way God does through His Word, His Son, and His Spirit. Only God can give new life and He has given the means of nourishment, growth, and change, without the assistance of man-made theories and therapies promoted throughout the twentieth century. The glorious truth about the Christian life is encapsulated in one short phrase: **"Christ in you, the hope of glory"** (Colossians 1:27).

Nevertheless, Smith contends that TheoPhostic counseling is God's gift, even though TheoPhostic is fully dependent on contradictory, secular psychological systems, theories, and techniques invented by people who rejected the God of the Bible and who were therefore people "having no hope" (Ephesians 2:12). These psychological systems usurp the central, authoritative, and exclusive place of the Word of God and work of the Holy Spirit in their surrogate attempts to explain and change the inner man.

Those who truly believe and live by the Gospel have opportunities to grow under duress unless they are distracted and waylaid by psychologically-based systems that may seem to help and heal but that will lead the person away from complete trust in the Lord and reliance on what He has provided for Christians since the inception of the church. Living by grace through faith in Christ and obedience to His Word, saints held steady throughout the centuries. Present-day forms of psychological manipulation may make one feel better temporarily but will not sustain one through the trials of life, especially those trials that test the faith to the degree experienced by those who suffered persecution and martyrdom. As one reads through the epistles, one sees how Christians were sustained by

God in the midst of suffering and how they could consider these sufferings "light affliction" when compared to the "eternal weight of glory" that would be theirs in eternity. In fact, the richness of the Christian life can increase through suffering as the person turns to God, rather than to the wisdom of the world, and as the person comes to know Him better by trusting Him through trials.

Besides looking forward to future glory in heaven, the believer looks to Jesus now, for Him to work His own good pleasure and to cause the believer to reflect His image more completely.

> But we all, with open face beholding as in a glass the glory of the Lord, are changed into the same image from glory to glory, even as by the Spirit of the Lord (2 Corinthians 3:18).

Jesus did not leave Christians without a source for help during problems of living. He supplies what is needed for every aspect of life.:

> If any man thirst, let him come unto me, and drink. He that believeth on me, as the Scripture hath said, out of his belly shall flow rivers of living water (John 7:37-38).

Jesus fulfills His promise to every believer, having sent the Holy Spirit to indwell believers and to enable them to live the new life He purchased for them through His death and resurrection. The Bible declares that believers have all they need for life and godliness in the sight of God (2 Peter 1).

The Bible is God's revelation about Himself and about the nature of man, how he is to live, and how he changes. TheoPhostic counseling cannot be considered divine because of its secular foundations. Neither is TheoPhostic counseling God's gift to Smith or His provision for Christians, since God has no need to rely on any psychological system invented by people who rejected His Son any more than He had to rely on the pagan gods of the nations around Israel. He does not need that kind of help because He is life and the source of life and well-being of every true Christian. The Christian is so completely connected to Jesus that Jesus compared His relationship to believers with that of a vine and its branches (John 15) and with that of a shepherd and his sheep (John 10). It is a relationship of profound love and intimacy. It is the oneness Jesus expressed in John 17, when he prayed:

> Neither pray I for these alone, but for them also which shall believe on me through their word; That they all may be one; as thou, Father, art in me, and I in thee, that they also may be one in us: that the world may believe that thou hast sent me . . . that the love wherewith thou has loved me may be in them, and I in them (John 17:20-21, 26).

What man-made system can compare with this opulent treasure of relationship with the Father and the Son. Even a brief moment of awareness of this awesome truth is far more glorious than all the promises of TheoPhostic counseling.

Those who have been devastated by disappointment, who have suffered pain inflicted by sinful humanity, and who seek an end to suffering even unto death will find genuine, everlasting help in Jesus. Why seek truth in the wisdom of men or sew man-made theories and methods together with the Bible in attempting to heal a soul when Christ has given truth, life, mercy and grace? Why go fossicking about in the past, trying to dredge up memories or dig up the old man from the grave, when Christ has given new life? Those who have been sinned against or who are in bondage to sin can only be set free by Jesus. All other methods of overcoming sin are superficial and temporary. Why mix the world's psychotherapies with God's promises when those indwelt by Jesus can walk by His life and His Word?

We encourage believers to seek God's face with diligence, put off the old (all that is of the world, the flesh, and the devil) and put on the new (all that is in Christ Jesus) when they are experiencing problems of living. He is faithful. "Let us therefore come boldly unto the throne of grace, that we may obtain mercy, and find grace to help in time of need" (Hebrews 4:16). Jesus gives true manna from heaven, rather than vain philosophies of men. He supplies springs of living water, not broken cisterns of psychological systems. Believers have a constant supply of help for each day as they walk in Christ Jesus rather than in the ways of the world. God's provision is sufficient, ample, and abundant.

Other EastGate Books by Martin and Deidre Bobgan

AGAINST "BIBLICAL COUNSELING": FOR THE BIBLE reveals what biblical counseling is, rather than what it pretends or even hopes to be. Its primary thrust is to call Christians back to the Bible and to biblically ordained ministries and mutual care in the Body of Christ. 200 pages, softbound, $12.

COMPETENT TO MINISTER: The Biblical Care of Souls calls Christians back to the Bible and to the biblically ordained ministries and mutual care in the Body of Christ, helps break down walls of intimidation that have hindered personal ministry among Christians, and presents the excellent, effective way believers can minister God's grace through biblical conversation, prayer, and practical help. 252 pages, softbound, $14.

CRI GUILTY OF PSYCHOHERESY? answers the CRI-Passantino "Psychology & the Church" series, exposes their illogical reasoning, and argues that supporting psychotherapy and its underlying psychologies is an opprobrium in the church. 152 pages, softbound, $10.

THE END OF "CHRISTIAN PSYCHOLOGY" reveals that "Christian psychology" includes contradictory theories and techniques; describes and analyzes major psychological theories influencing Christians; presents evidence to show that professional psychotherapy with its underlying psychologies is questionable at best, detrimental at worst, and a spiritual counterfeit at least; and challenges the church to rid itself of all signs and symptoms of this scourge. 290 pages, softbound, $14.

FOUR TEMPERAMENTS, ASTROLOGY & PERSONALITY TESTING examines personality types and tests from a biblical, historical, and research basis. 214 pages, soft-bound, $12.

JAMES DOBSON'S GOSPEL OF SELF-ESTEEM & PSYCHOLOGY clearly demonstrates that some of Dobson's basic assumptions and many of his specific teachings originated from secular psychological theorists whose opinions are based on godless foundations. Self-esteem and psychology are the two major thrusts of his ministry that supersede sin, salvation, and sanctification. They are another gospel. 248 pages, softbound, $15.

LARRY CRABB'S GOSPEL traces Crabb's 22-year journey of jolts, shifts, and expansions as he has sought to create the best combination of psychology and the Bible. While on the surface Crabb's books progressively sound more biblical, his eclectic theories and methods remain psychologically bound and consistent with current psychotherapy trends. This book provides a detailed analysis of Crabb's psychotheology. 210 pages, softbound $12.

PSYCHOHERESY: The Psychological Seduction of Christianity exposes fallacies and failures of psychological counseling theories and therapies for one purpose: to call the church back to the Word of God and the work of the Holy Spirit. Besides revealing the anti-Christian biases, internal contradictions, and documented failures of secular psychotherapy, it examines various amalgamations of secular psychologies with Christianity and explodes firmly entrenched myths that undergird these unholy unions. 272 pages, softbound, $15.

12 STEPS TO DESTRUCTION: Codependency/Recovery Heresies examines codependency/recovery teachings, Alcoholics Anonymous, twelve-step groups, and addiction treatment programs from a biblical, historical, and research perspective and urges believers to trust in the sufficiency of Christ and the Word of God. 256 pages, softbound, $12.